David Algar could best be described as a 'middle class itinerant', always moving from school to school and place to place. His first degree, from Aberystwyth University, was in Economics and International Relations; forty years later, he completed a second degree in Psychology and Politics. The wandering life included a long career in industry, regularly changing jobs in the nick of time to avoid being found out.

Along the way, he has managed to pick up a wife, two kids and five chickens, three bikes and a kayak, all to be found in a small village in South Buckinghamshire. Writing came late in life, fuelled by the curiosity brought on by being continually on the move: a curiosity for how we live through the chaos in the world, how we use our humanity for good and how we can all – especially men – be immensely silly along the way.

When he's not writing, or gazing into the middle distance, David is happiest travelling, playing sport or just being badly behaved with friends.

MAN TROUBLE

David Algar

Constellations Press

First published in 2023
by Constellations Press

Typeset by Constellations Press

Printed and bound in the UK by Biddles, Kings Lynn

A CIP record for this book is available from the British Library

ISBN 978-1-917000-00-0
eISBN 978-1-917000-10-9

*I knew it was going to be a bad day when I played Pooh Sticks
against myself and neither stick came through.*

David (aged 288 months)

Contents

Foreword	xi
Masculinity: a User's Guide	13
Why Do We Bother?	21
Am I Alone?	27
On Friendship and Loneliness	29
The Challenges of Owning a Willy	37
Malos Muchachos: the Essence of a Boys' Trip	43
Hang On Snoopy, Snoopy Hang On!	49
Drinking Culture and the Culture of Drinking	51
Transitioning	59
Giving Ourselves a Sporting Chance	65
Fathers and Sons	75
Men and the Patriarchy	81
Why do my Glasses keep going Off-Grid?	85
The Tyranny of the Bow	87
IT and Me	89
Men and Women: Mars and Venus, or Just around the Corner?	95

The Pecking Order	107
Nicknames and Banter	109
Political Correctness and Humour: an Incomplete Reflection	115
I Bear-Sprayed the Dog	123
Cancer: Diagnosis and the Worst Bit	127
Cancer: the Treatment	135
Cancer: the Epilogue	149
Ziggy	153
Heaven Can Wait	159
Tribal Man	161
Politics: Left! Right! Left! Right! Left…?	173
Tilting at Windmills	185
Buying a Watch Really Shouldn't be this Difficult	189
The Peacock Whisperer	193
I Want a Viking Burial	197
Useful Reading	201

Foreword

This book – part confessional, part social analysis – aims to balance two conflicting ideas. On one hand, it wants men to take themselves more seriously so they can understand their role in the world and thus protect their mental, physical and emotional health – things that are at risk if the world is allowed a free run at them. On the other hand, it exhorts men not to take themselves too seriously and to accept that they think and do dumb things from time to time – things that are the inevitable result of being human in an immensely complex world. Some of the essays address masculinity itself, and engage with what it means to be a man in our society. Others are more personal and speak to my own experience of just being human, as well as male. Some are serious and represent my deep engagement with the social issues that trouble me; others are meant to be funny, to open a window on the life and thoughts of a late-middle-aged bloke – who at his time of life should be better behaved.

I hope that these essays will stimulate ideas, provoke disagreement and make you laugh.

David Algar • June 2023

Masculinity: a User's Guide

'The happiest man is the one who is closest to his outward image.' This is something that was taught to me by my school counsellor, Mrs Mair-Thomas, and it probably took me forty-odd years to understand it fully. It reflects on masculinity, the pressures to conform to an image, what it is to be a man and how men might achieve some kind of peace and harmony in their lives.

I'm a man, which arguably gives me a bit of a head start in understanding masculinity, and I also come from a position of liking being a man. I have deep sympathy for anyone who is not comfortable in their original sexuality but I am lucky in that I kind of fit with what nature had in store for me. However, even as someone who was born a boy and who turned into a man, it's hard to articulate what masculinity means, except that you know it is important. It's like asking a fish why it swims or a flower why it faces the sun. It's simply what we are, how we think and how we act. It's also an artificial social construct, in that masculine traits are defined by what men and women expect masculinity to be, and how society expects masculinity to express itself. By society, I mean the institutions, histories, social structures and individual relationships that make up our daily lives, some mandatory and some voluntary, but in which no man, nor woman, can be an island. Masculinity will mean different things to different people, with divergent and equally legitimate emphases on traits and values. These differences might range from subtle to obvious displays, and how they are received will be important – amplified by the relationship between masculinity and femininity which is fascinatingly complex, and often expressed in terms of binary opposition i.e. exhibiting commonly accepted female traits defines what makes a man and vice versa, in the same way that hot is not cold and happy is not sad.

Growing up in the 1970s was not a 'woke' or sensitive experience. At least, it didn't seem to be for me or my contemporaries – though to a degree we were all acting. We grew up with hairy-chested film stars and aftershave adverts that encouraged us to wear the 'mark of a man' or to surf a tubing wave. To this day, I feel ever so slightly inferior for not having a hairy chest and I still can't surf to save my life. Girls, while being fascinating and a little scary, were the subject of male conquests; snogging as many girls as possible pushed you up the masculinity scale. Sport was another way to burnish your credentials as a man, especially if fighting could become part of it – the perfect combination for rugby and, living in South Wales, you were considered 'gay' if you didn't play. With hindsight, I can see that as a shameful attitude but at the time we didn't interrogate what it was to be gay; it was just a concept against which to define heterosexual masculinity. A spin-off of this was hazardous drinking, which we practised two or three times a week. Masculinity, as we experienced it, was aggressive, competitive and 'worn on our sleeves', and we never considered that there were other types. In the language of Bonnie Tyler, who was apparently 'holding out for a hero', we needed to arrive on a 'fiery steed', be a 'streetwise Hercules' and be 'fresh from the fight' – completely ignoring how difficult it was to get 'fiery steeds' at that time in South Wales. The quieter, more thoughtful, maybe stronger guys, or even gay men, all had their own type of maleness – it just didn't occur to us to explore it. On top of doing all the 'boy stuff', we had to operate in a 'big boys don't cry' atmosphere of self-reliance and apparent inner strength. Boys were risk-takers: tough, competitive, aggressive and part of the male tribe, and you didn't fuck with the tribe – because if you did fuck with the tribe, you lost your social anchors and, for young people particularly, you desperately needed to belong. We were boys, barely men, trying to understand our bodies and minds at a hugely unstable time in life, when hormones were coursing through us. Masculinity was an obvious hook to grab and it gave us relatively simple rules of engagement, irrespective of whether it suited our values and interests. It was the powerful drug that anaesthetised rational thought processes. It was also addictive in that it was hard to break away, unless you had the courage to challenge the tribe – thereby risking loneliness and isolation. Eventually, I learned that being punched in the face wasn't much fun; drinking until you threw up wasn't a great use of money or energy; and girls were actually quite interesting to talk to. It took me a while to get there, with a slow evolution well into my twenties, in part because the pressures of perceived masculinity were so pervasive.

Masculinity today is similarly fluid and tricky to pin down and interpret. It can be the superficial cloak that we wear to advertise our maleness, or it can be the deep structural essence of the person. In the second of these we may recognise a wholly different manifestation of the masculine: from the macho to the effete; the highly competitive to the self-sacrificing and compassionate; the logical problem-solver to the gentle family provider. We can see it in a man who can run into a burning building or stand up to injustice with the power of his intellect and decency, while we are only too aware of the dark, manipulative and predatory nature masculinity can present. Masculinity can manifest itself in many ways and society's judgement will be important because it will impact on the way individuals see themselves – a cyclical process reinforcing behavioural norms for good or ill: good because men are responsible for some of humanity's great leaps forward; and ill because they are also responsible for some of history's most appalling acts.

My views on masculinity have changed as I have aged, and life has served up many lessons, but also because societal pressures have changed. We lived through the 'new man' of the nineties experience but that was just a curtain raiser for today's attitudes. Masculinity has softened and become more thoughtful. Mainstream feminism has pushed back on some of the worst excesses, and society has challenged some of the masculine hegemony. Attitudinal changes and digital economies have opened up different jobs, while our communities have evolved to incorporate greater equality of opportunity – women and girls are now able to compete more fairly and are giving the male sex a run for its money. I would now define masculinity in a very different way than my younger self would have done. It should be about: taking responsibility for ourselves and our world; having the courage to do what is right and, if necessary, fight with our bodies, our minds and our decency; living with drive, energy and, yes, competitiveness; and incorporating some of the protector and provider qualities that nature has gifted us. No doubt, we will continue to exhibit whatever helps with sexual attraction and some version of *Love Island* man is perhaps inescapable – it just shouldn't be taken too seriously. It should be stressed that these characteristics are not exclusive to men but they do represent a view of masculinity at this point in time.

Much of the experience of being human pivots on our individual relationships, which are inevitably influenced by the social mores of the time – our ideas about ourselves, including how masculinity is understood, are fluid, subject to change and vulnerable to influence. We inhabit the world as individuals, but our relationships can also have a life of their own, and, in turn, have an impact on how men behave. They are extraordinarily complex to articulate, and investigating these relationships is like observing and trying to understand the confluence of two rivers. The rivers may be silted or clear, colder or warmer, fast-flowing or meandering and will be influenced by earlier tributaries that have flowed in. Good luck analysing the new river, except to say that there is now a different entity, with origins in its two constituent parts, but with whole new levels of complexity. Specifically, our key relationships with life partners adds a whole new dimension to masculinity. Most of us move from clumsy fumblers through wild oats spreaders to responsible parents and providers, although divorce and single parenting change family dynamics in very complicated ways. We tend to have families and children that require better behaviour of us as men, but importantly we also now have another tribe to hook up to – a self-made, small family tribe. Our partners can soften and hold a mirror up to unacceptable masculinity, so that continual influence and the pressures of life should make us better men – because we have responsibilities. We need the security and experiences that relationships bring, trumping the sexual drives of our younger selves. The shorthand for this is companionship. Clearly, I'm expressing generalities here – good and bad can happen at both ends of the spectrum and, even in the middle of the bell curve, life is highly complex, fraught and exceptional.

Teachers, role models, values-based education and social or legal pressures are crucial, but men, in general, will be greater risk-takers and more competitive creatures. In the future, it's highly unlikely that prison populations will reflect a fifty-fifty split or that young men will stop doing daft or dangerous things. I wonder if we will ever equalise the male bias towards science, technology or maths subjects in schools. Will men ever match up to the caring and nurturing qualities of women – and, indeed, would they naturally want to? Will women make up half of our armed forces or focus on other more dangerous jobs in the future – and, indeed, would they naturally want to? If, in broad terms, you accept different traits, or emphasis of characteristics, between the sexes, is there a danger that we force-fit expectations that don't come naturally? What is important, though, is that both men and women have the opportunities to follow where their personalities, skills and preferences lead.

As generally defined, 'maleness' refers to the biological, evolutionary and physical nature of being a man. Men are a product of their bodies, hormones and inherent personality traits and, over thousands of years, have evolved to handle different survival and procreation challenges. Masculinity, however, brings a new dimension to maleness, by adding the social expectations and practices of manhood that most of us recognise. As men, we are driven by what is expected of us as well as what is deep within us. The biological effect is easier to measure but how does one assess the influences of the world about us? How can we isolate family upbringing, school, teachers, friends, job choices, health problems, the media and a host of other factors? Psychologists and sociologists have been able to articulate meaningful themes and can now isolate the causes of some key behaviours with a degree of success – things like delinquency, academic achievement (or failure) and social isolation. However, it's still akin to introducing more fruit and vegetables into a diet and trying to prove the effect on general wellbeing.

In short, there is no universal definition of masculinity and it varies by geography, historical epoch, social class, age, and race, as well as the individual's psychological make-up. Add to these the perception of those who experience male behaviour and you have the complexities and contradictions that embody masculinity. There are, however, broad themes that are worth studying and articulating if we are to achieve better outcomes. One of these themes is how we reconcile external norms of masculinity with the nature of the inner man – bringing him 'closest to his outward image'. If the image and reality are too dissonant, something that is true for men and women, people can develop significant mental and physical health problems. These undermine individual fulfilment, lead to unhappy people and suck resources out of our healthcare systems.

Why Do We Bother?

Every so often I get profound 'existential anxiety' or, put more simply, I ask, 'What the fuck are we doing here?'

I look at strangers, acquaintances and loved ones and I can't really know what it's like to be them, and they can't really know what it's like to be me. Eight billion people are wandering around this planet with a unique experience of what it's like to inhabit their body and their mind. How we experience pain or joy may be different, or we may just see the colour blue when others see our version of red. As we draw the focus closer to ourselves with our families and our children, who are the most comparable, we see patterns that we can identify and start to understand. We make the intuitive leap that a certain set of behaviours represents a certain set of thoughts and feelings but we can never know for sure. Even our children have different characteristics and personality facets, as well as influences from the external environment.

I don't sit here wringing my hands, worried that we could be judging our fellow humans wrongly – I suspect we will have it pretty well right, given the multiple contacts with our fellow man. What I do recognise is that we all start from a basis of 'unique aloneness' and life gets built on this. Our lives are constructed around a potentially overwhelming concept of the 'self' with the extraordinary weight of our own responsibility to survive and thrive. Most of us learn to live with this responsibility and develop social, mental and emotional structures that make life good and valuable. However, if these structures are not in place or are weakened or are significantly out of balance, the 'unique aloneness' becomes a rock showing above the waterline – a rock that can catch and hurt us as we float or swim downstream.

The counterbalances to our aloneness are joy and fulfilment, but also the simple life force that is in us all. This, in most cases, supersedes the profound weaknesses of the human condition. It makes us take responsibility for ourselves and build a life, whatever the hand that we're dealt. It enables us to withstand emotional and physical pain and still continue to put one foot in front of the other. Driven by this, individual lives and social structures have extraordinary momentum and power to go forward. Yet, for 5,224 people in England and Wales in 2020, that energy wasn't strong enough to stop them taking their own lives. It's impossible to generalise about the circumstances that lead someone to make such a desperate decision, but I suspect that many of us will have intimations of the events or circumstances that could push us down that path; we all experience pain and hopelessness at some time. It's relevant, though, to highlight that three quarters of these suicides were men. The largest age group for suicide is 45-49 for both men and women, but it's the biggest killer of young men under thirty. These figures are tragic in isolation, but it's also worth remembering that they represent the end of a spectrum: a large number of people are likely to feel some of this pain, some of the time. We ignore mental health at our peril. Not only will early intervention and understanding save some lives but their effect on the wellbeing of millions can be incredibly powerful.

If life force and profound aloneness define us, we also live with many paradoxes as part of the human condition. We outsource some of our happiness to a partner whom we choose out of a pool of a few hundred people, not the whole eight billion. Looking for someone to fit our personality and needs is a hugely inefficient game of lucky dip. We're trying to identify someone who is complementary to us, emotionally, intellectually and sexually, and who has the same life expectations – all wrapped up in that elusive concept of 'love'. Oh, and, of course, needs and circumstances change with age and experience, so it's even more of a moving target. Then, as intelligent adults, we bring children into this world, in the certain knowledge that they will suffer pain and unhappiness to go alongside the hoped-for joy and fulfilment – and we pay for it at considerable cost, sacrifice and a lifetime of worry. If we did a proper cost/benefit analysis, would we still do it? Fortunately, it would be over-ruled by our natures and the innate drive to perpetuate the species – together with our need for purpose and meaning.

We take career decisions with about the same amount of due diligence we deploy in looking for love. Of course, many people are happy and stimulated but many others are struggling, bored and miserable in their jobs. Could I have found my metier as a cowboy or could I have gone down the medical path and been a danger to my fellow citizens?

Then, of course, there is the absolutely unavoidable concept of death – we only get a certain amount of time, even if we are lucky enough to escape serious illness and accident along the way. It's in our minds right from childhood, but we can't afford to engage with it too much, because therein lies madness. It's a subject that's even more terrifying because it will happen to our families, friends and, most appallingly of all, to our children – the best we can hope for is that it follows a natural path and we don't have to bury someone significantly younger than us.

Despite these paradoxes and deep characteristics, humans are brilliant at creating structures to alleviate the bad and release the profound joy and fulfilment that is out there: we build families, friendships, villages, nations and connections that protect and nurture; we learn to live, with some harmony, in the incredible beauty and ferocity of nature, on our one and only planet; we establish extraordinary emotional relationships and then devise all sorts of rituals to reinforce and protect them; and we train our minds to cope – learning from our parents and peers and the plethora of self-help information on groaning bookshelves.

We even build structures to reconcile the contradictory demands of purpose, death and the afterlife. Organised religion and individual spirituality feature in all cultures and are seemingly deeply human. 'What comes first' is a debate on which I feel ill-equipped to comment. Is there a force or being beyond our experience that put us here or – something we have form for – do we build artificial structures to reconcile the irreconcilable? I'm keeping my options open, but I do want to believe in the beauty and good I see around me, and I hope it's a reason for being.

I'm acutely aware that I write from a privileged, Western European perspective, while billions live at the bottom of the Maslovian hierarchy – struggling for food and shelter and without the luxury of time to consider existential angst. There are also millions who are seriously disadvantaged by the state of their mental and physical health, the environment in which they live, and the aggressive, expansionist behaviour of others – things we could fix if we chose to. Yet, everywhere, we see the same life forces and paradoxes at play, alongside the same type of social structures; the eight billion club, made up of eight billion unique and solitary individuals, is still very much in operation.

So, why do we bother to stay in this world and why, more tragically, might we choose not to? I think we stay, in large part, because it's what we are designed to do. It's the animal in us that needs to survive and cling to our bit of rock. The human in us will try to understand and improve our lot, but the animal instinct that underpins our behaviour is extraordinarily powerful. We are hardwired to want to live and to find ways of doing it. The good in our world is an incredible force, even though we know that evil is demonstrably out there. Our social and emotional lives can be incredibly joyful and fulfilling, hopefully more than compensating for the pain that will inevitably come. There is heart-stopping beauty to love, but we can also expect to encounter the ugly on our journey. And we have fantastic brains to think ourselves out of trouble, though, sadly, also to think ourselves into trouble. Finally, there may be a sporting chance of something at the end of life, although, if it's nothing, I believe that a life well-lived is a purpose in itself – I just hope that if there is a god out there, they will be tolerant of my curious and questioning mind.

Am I Alone?

This is a tribute to Billy Connolly, who exhorted us to 'seek the company of people who, when left alone with a tea cosy, will always try it on'. It provoked me to research the degree of silliness that is out there, indulged in when no one is watching – typically, though not exclusively, more of a boy thing (the inner child in us is often peeping out, looking for fun). This is clearly evidenced by the 'fan test' – I've never met a woman who has stuck her finger in a spinning fan, yet most men I know have tried it, with varying degrees of collateral damage. This discussion also led to a fruitful and exciting WhatsApp conversation, with people competing to wear the best tea cosy.

So, who hasn't pointed a single banana at the dog and, drawing on their inner James Cagney, said, 'Stick 'em up, you dirty rat'? This manoeuvre also entertains in the greengrocers, though you tend to get gently ushered out of the shop – sometimes with a free banana. A shower head is the perfect microphone for singing Bryan Adams' songs to the hundreds of thousands of fans who happen to be in your bathroom. A tennis racket can put you on stage with Status Quo or, on a bad day, by a river in the Deep South doing *Duelling Banjos* to the bewilderment of the locals. One friend has admitted that he has put his wife's stockings over his head to see what it's like to be a bank robber; his wife is still cross with him. My fifty-year-old brother-in-law, having too much time on his hands, suddenly shaved all his pubic hair off just to see what it was like – then was unhappy because chicken giblets are never a good look. Only the very brave would admit to surprising a sleeping partner by rolling their nipples between his forefingers and thumbs, leaning in and saying 'London calling! London calling! – can you hear me, London?' You need to be in a very long term and indulgent relationship to get away with this. Finally, I'll end with my favourite example: another friend who admits to putting a bra on his head and strapping it under his chin like Biggles' helmet – while humming the theme tune to *The Dam Busters*.

Come on! We've all done it! Haven't we?

On Friendship and Loneliness

Friendship and loneliness are two social constructs that are inextricably linked, because they address our need to belong and because they express our common humanity. They are clearly complex subjects, but I would contend that understanding them will have a material impact on well-being within society. I've been incredibly lucky with friends, but I've only learned to appreciate them fully after a period of crushing loneliness.

I have a couple of long-standing friends from school, identified under the WhatsApp group 'Clinging to the Wreckage', so named (with our typical gallows humour) because a couple of us have had life-threatening illnesses. We have so much shared history that any irritations or annoyances are easily forgiven. We've supported each other through growing into adulthood, marriage breakdowns, mental health issues and numerous job changes – and we've had fun together, a lot of fun. I often wonder whether we would become so close if we met now but the ties of time and experience go deep. We've known each other at our most vulnerable and prattish, so, when we are together, there really is no point trying to be something we are not. Old friends safeguard the version of who you were, and the journey you have taken to get to the present.

There are also friends from university, though we can often

go months or years without seeing each other. Most recently, we cycled together to Istanbul, a journey of great joys and great challenges, on which we faced situations that tested our friendship to the limit. Once again, a shared history – including experiences involving personal tragedy and some profound mental and physical crises – was the powerful bond that kept us together. Normally, we just meet up in South Wales, talk bollocks and get drunk, but whatever the circumstances, we slip back easily into a comfortable relationship of taking the piss – with jokes that have hardly changed in forty years. We've got many skeletons in our cupboards, we've shared the good things in life and we have deep knowledge of each other's pain – things that we recognise and make allowances for and which make our friendship so vital.

Then, over the years, I've just accidentally collected friends, some of whom I suddenly realise I've known for three decades. We've travelled large parts of the world together, set up successful businesses, been there for each other in difficult times and taken our ageing bodies through experiences designed for the young and foolish. Interestingly, new friends in later life are different, partly because they are not forged in history. The relationships can still have banter and messing around, but they seem a bit more grown up. They operate in the present, because the present is where they come from; inevitably the tenor and emotional register of these friendships are more adult in nature. This can be very good, of course, but I often feel I'm presenting myself against the background of a socially manufactured set of rules. I'm what people expect me to be now, because I'm a father, doing a job, getting grey hairs, or whatever – but when I'm with my older friends I can also relax into my younger self, without the many labels associated with who I am today.

And, let me make it clear, in all the above relationships, we don't do compliments – from anyone, to anyone. We might say thank you, but most of the time we are just rude to each other, in our happy 'dog-eat-dog' world. The best you might get is 'You played well today – for a fat bloke'. But if you are in that 'mates' world', you are in a great place, and you are accepted even if you are crap at banter, or can be a plonker at times. Your mates are there to keep your feet on the ground, which is caring in a very oblique way. So, before this turns into *West Side Story*, I've highlighted all the above because they represent friendships and friendships are what keep me sane.

In case I sound too one-dimensional, I do have many women friends, and two special sisters, but the relationships are always slightly different. Probably they are a lot more mature and thoughtful, certainly they are less blokeish, but they are still fun – even if these friends don't share my desire to build a beach volleyball court in a muddy field.

We are all a product of our experiences and we learn hard lessons along the way. I went through a miserable period of loneliness when I was sixteen or seventeen, and I never want to feel that again. I went from being 'one of the boys' in one school to being utterly isolated in the next. I knew no-one, was unsure of who I was and my self-confidence was shot full of holes – while all around me people seemed to be popular and sorted. In school, I'd pretend to read a book or even continually reorganise the inside of my desk. Breaks were a nightmare; the loneliness just projected off me. I spent the time trying to look busy or as if I had somewhere to go. After lunch, I'd walk out of school to a small wooded area and just sit on a branch until it was safe to go back into lessons.

On top of this, my course choice was really messy, having

done the wrong O-Levels – all sciences. A blind, crazy man on a wild horse could see that I was never going to be a scientist. I remember sitting in an Advanced Maths lesson on quadratic equations, failing to understand a single word from beginning to end; I didn't even understand why I needed to understand.

Loneliness is a peculiar, complex cocktail of emotions, or it certainly was in my case. There is embarrassment first and foremost: embarrassment that you don't have any friends and embarrassment that you can't function as a social animal, like everyone else. Then there's anger: anger that you've been put in this situation, and anger with yourself that you can't work your way out of it. There is also the feeling of being overwhelmed: a shocking understanding that this is just life, and you're going to have to plot a course through a minefield of social and practical difficulties. I distinctly recall irrationally envying my grandparents who were reaching the end of their lives, and were no longer suffering the fear and self-loathing that I was facing. That is probably the nearest I came to suicidal thoughts, but I can understand how people get themselves into that bad situation – it must be the lack of hope or a never-ending vortex that sucks your life chances away. Loneliness is a combination of all of the above but it's also a sick feeling, deep in your stomach. Guts are twisted and they feel dark red and black and angry purple. Your mind is racing too fast, and you're exhausted – tired to your bones. And you're sure no-one else knows what you're going through, because this is what it's like to be uniquely, and profoundly, vulnerable.

I came through it and I'm still here, but I was changed by the experience and my innocence was lost. Now I can see that it afforded me some useful life lessons, but it was a process that hurt so much – the corners of my being kept catching on life and the inner core was barely able to function, let alone like itself. The school worked out that something was wrong and, thank goodness, put me together with my lovely, but no-nonsense, counsellor – Mrs Mair-Thomas – whom I will always remember. Thanks to her influence, I started to make friends, with people who had the grace to include me and give me a chance, even though in my mental state I was trying too hard, and could be a real dick. The gang that was to become the 'Clinging to the Wreckage' group, all these years later, took me under their wing. I really don't know why this happened, except that perhaps my true personality was starting to emerge from the swamp – and they responded to it. Plus, of course, they had their own vulnerabilities and emotional needs that my tormented state failed to recognise. Finally, I sorted out my A-Level courses and got picked for the rugby team, so I started to feel on more solid ground.

Notwithstanding all this, I made one more visit to my place in the woods, just as I was emerging into a different and happier state of mind. It was a kind of homage to a place of safety, which maybe we all need. I sat still for around twenty minutes and I have no recollection of what was going through my mind. But what I do remember was that a robin flew up and landed on my knee. We both sat there for thirty seconds and then it was gone. Possibly it was a sign, but probably just a coincidence, though to this day, forty odd years later, the thought still catches me out.

I profoundly hate the idea of anyone else being lonely which makes me hypersensitive to it. I pick up waifs and strays all the time, especially in social or work settings. It doesn't always end well, and you can get stuck with people you have nothing in common with, but I feel that I have no choice, given my experience.

As humans, we have to live in our own heads, making

loneliness even more dangerous. We have all sorts of questions, chief among them: do other people think like this? Our minds contain extraordinarily complex menus where the tastes and colours of the individual ingredients are difficult to discern; yet sometimes we have to distinguish them, so we can understand and make sense of ourselves – friends help us do this. If we can do this alone, great, but I'd contend that most of us need others to give us perspective. If we are alone, we run the risk of unravelling.

Loneliness is also a social problem as well as a psychological and personal one. In 2020, an academic study demonstrated the long-term growth of loneliness in Western society (Hertz, 2020), suggesting the rise has been caused by the movement from rural to urban areas, the breakdown of family units, the changing nature of work and the effect of technology on our lives. This is especially frightening when we see the breakdown of close communities and a rapid, and apparently inexorable, movement towards a globalised world. People need to belong to groups, because without that connection they can become isolated which can lead to despair and rage. This is not to underestimate the benefits of being able to communicate instantly to anyone around the globe. But it's a dramatically different experience of society than even thirty or forty years ago – which, in evolutionary terms, is just a blink of an eye. People are expected to adapt at an astonishing pace and there is always the risk that human relationships become collateral damage. However, we now have the chance to engage with like-minded people from a massive pool of over eight billion, rather than the thirty-five who happen to be in our school year group. That has to be an opportunity for connecting humanity, albeit not without its risks.

Mental health has rightly come to the forefront of our

attention in recent years. It impacts on our physical health and our economic well-being, and has a huge cost to both individuals and society. Loneliness can be a part of this and the good news is it's fixable. It's not like an incurable cancer, where we only have palliative care. People experience loneliness for a number of different reasons – job changes, health problems, grieving – or no reason at all: sometimes your mind just dislocates in some way. It can affect young and old, poor and rich, and (most frightening of all) you don't always see it coming. As a teenager it happened to me out of nowhere, and at a time when I lacked the intellectual, social or emotional tools to either understand or cope. It was brutal, but it was part of the human condition that can affect anyone at any life stage – so if we recognise and call it for what it is we, maybe, have a chance of alleviate it.

Although loneliness affects many people, it nevertheless remains a condition loaded with negative associations and stigma. It's something that is not cool to admit to and government initiatives are fighting to be heard. At best, we try to encourage citizenship and neighbourhood engagement but it's a mental health issue as well as social. So, it's down to the brave, or the unembarrassed, to do something about it. Find an excuse to call a friend, chat to a work colleague, and ask some open questions. Send someone something that you think would be uniquely relevant to them and make them feel special. Organise a kick-about in the park or a gin-tasting session. Get a regular event going, like a bike ride or a model railway club. Deliberately bump into a neighbour and just start to talk. Look for the signs of isolation, but recognise that someone else may be a better conduit than you to help – and put these people together.

If you are feeling lonely, as many of us will in our lives, do the same. Get out there and try things. Maybe join a club, learn a language, do a weekly park run, volunteer in your community. You don't have to be good at something, just engage – then things happen, though probably not in the way you expect. In my experience, it's rarely a straight-line process but, just by joining in with the world, you become open to others and they respond. If someone suggests going for a coffee, do it – they probably didn't ask because they felt they should, but, even if they did, remember that their compassion is born out of kindness and concern. You are worthy of other people's friendship and the more you are yourself, the more you will find like-minded people. The hippy in me believes in a kind of 'nature-designed' karma, where the real version of ourselves connects with our designated part of the world – when we are open to those connections.

Finally, remember that everyone makes mistakes in navigating complex human relationships, so be prepared to keep trying. You may be clumsy with someone you were trying to help or you may find you hate parkruns with a passion, but at least you tried. And keep trying: something, anything. Ask for help when you need it, and give help when you can, because alleviating loneliness is one of the rare things in life that works both ways. It's a good thing to do; we all, deep down, understand it, and we may be grateful for that awareness as we blunder though our own lives.

The Challenges of Owning a Willy

For most men, having a willy is of lifelong interest, so why not explore the relationship further? There is always a danger that this might turn into a version of the 1980s *Wicked Willie* stories, but, however formative and entertaining they were, let's hope not.

In general terms, for boys growing up, the willy starts as a thing of interest because half of the population doesn't have one – so the assumption is it has to be a bit special. It then emerges that it is rude, so, from a small boy's viewpoint, this is just brilliant, with huge scope for silly names and sniggering.

After the rude stage, it gets even more fun as it starts to change and does things you never imagined possible. You spend most of your teenage years with an erection, even if you are stuck in a geography lesson or outside picking up litter. At this point, the reason the other half of the population doesn't have one starts to fall into place and a lifelong obsession is born.

I guess your 20s and 30s are the heydays for the willy and your joint relationship. It's confident, it's brash and it always works on demand. It's also learned new tricks, which may or may not be good news for the willy-less half of society.

By the time you get to your 40s, having a willy is a bit like being an ageing rock star. You have to be prepared to live off former glories; it can be brought out for chat shows and royal events, and is always good for a greatest hits set. At this stage, it's best not to try new material as the crowd won't thank you for it. They prefer to know all the words and will understand if the performances are spread out a bit more – in reality, they will probably be rather grateful for that.

In your 50s, genetically speaking, you are pretty lucky to be around. As primitive man, at this age, the chances are that you'd be at the back of the cave hoping for scraps – unless of course you'd had the sense to retrain as cave painters or soothsayers at an earlier date. You sure as hell wouldn't be ripping bearskins off young, unsuspecting females, who would have better gene-pool contributors to consider. So, against this depressing historical backdrop, it may be considered nice to still be in the game.

Beyond this, I have no first-hand experience, other than to suspect that it doesn't end well. One of the worst parts must be that it's hanging there as a constant reminder – a sort of deflated space hopper stuck in the back of the garage, reminding you of fun-packed summer days. While there may still be a residual memory of the past, its main function is to get you up three times in the night.

At least most of us get buried with it, though it may have had tubes stuck up it in the final lap; sitting here in my late middle age, I'm already starting to worry about such indignity.

In conclusion, and given its constantly changing nature, is it any wonder my gender chooses to check on it on a regular basis – probably every half an hour or so? Regular inventory-taking is just a bloke thing, and no amount of explaining to the willy-less group will ever change that – something might just have fallen off!

And now for the more specific personal experience. From

a very early age, mine chose to exert a disproportionate and turbulent influence on my life. Apparently, and my memory is sketchy, I was diagnosed with too tight a foreskin – sadly not because I was hung like a horse. The four stitches I had to endure have been cleverly blocked out of my mind but I do remember the salt baths afterwards – sitting naked in the washing-up bowl on the kitchen floor. These sorts of things can scar a boy and the memory is deep.

The next eight or ten years were relatively uneventful. I'm sure I occasionally showed mine to a girl who promised to show me hers, but nothing to get me on the Sex Offenders Register. The foreskin problem was fixed and, with complete lack of sexual awareness, I continued to wear M&S Y-Fronts.

Then came the puberty years. And the underpants had to improve. This is the time when the relationship between a boy and his willy is at its most critical, constantly shifting as it does between deep love and profound insecurity: love, because of all the nice things that you can do with it – without having to dress for the occasion or make small talk; insecurity, because you're not sure that it is behaving normally and you have no idea whether it's the right size or shape. Early porn stars like King Dong didn't help, and please remember, dear reader, that this was well before the age of internet searches. The *Encyclopaedia Britannica* offered no insights, and you sure as hell weren't going to discuss it with your mates. These things prey on the mind of teenage boys.

At about the age of thirteen or fourteen, there was something of a crisis – not helped by the fashion for excruciatingly tight jeans. My mother and my sister used to bounce me into mine and then watch me strut down the road like a Rick Parfitt impersonator who was unable to bend at the knee. After a couple of weeks, I started to get real problems, which my mother just put down to 'growing pains' – failing to make the link with the jeans entry strategy. Thank God my dad had the sense to take me straight down to the doctors; by that afternoon I was in hospital awaiting emergency surgery for a suspected twisted testicle. I got poked around rather too much and then a nurse shaved off the few bits of pubic hair I had so proudly been growing – bizarrely preparing the area with talcum powder, which, in those days, was the answer to most problems. Then, for some inexplicable reason, a doctor drew the curtains around me and told me to lie on my side, with my knees to my chest. I should have known something was up when she put on a rubber glove, but nothing could prepare me for the pain and indignity of her sticking a finger up my bum – without so much as a warning or, at least, dinner first. My blood-curdling scream was witnessed by the ward, together with most of Carshalton, and I decided then and there that homosexuality was not an option. If I ever get advanced prostate cancer, it will be that doctor's fault, as even now I still come out in a cold sweat at the thought of anyone going near my bum. Then, it was down to the operating theatre, where a mischievous young doctor asked me what I thought of all the 'pretty nurses'. I'm confident they found out what my thoughts were under anaesthetic, but I have often wondered what type of sweepstake they had running.

When I woke, it had all been a bit of a false alarm, but a thorough inventory was still very much in order. The doctor had already promised me that I could 'still fire on one cylinder' and that I'd get a false one if necessary but it was still a massive relief to execute a full count. This relief was tempered by the ridiculous contraption that they'd put me in. The bald budgie was sticking out of a hole in a kind of strap-on device, looking like the primitive sanitary protection product teenage girls had to endure. The ball sack was pink, for goodness' sake – what marketing manager in medical supplies could possibly have thought that bright pink was an appropriate colour for a product that could only be used with a pair of testicles?

So, I left hospital intact, balls encased in pink, and having learned how to shuffle and cheat at cards from the old guy in the next bed. I then had to go back into school, expecting to have to explain my absence. The loaded silence made it clear that they had all been briefed to ask no questions, which, in a mixed class, was doubly embarrassing. I kept the pink ball sack for several years as a kind of trophy and, to this day, I still wear tight trousers.

My later teenage years were fumbling and awkward, given that any guidance came from stolen copies of *Mayfair* and *Confessions of a Window Cleaner*. The women in those glossy magazines bore little relationship to the girls in my class, and the possibility of horny housewives seducing me as I climbed my ladder would have scared the shit out of me. In those days, a glimpse of a bra strap or crossed legs would give me a week's worth of fantasies. Girls really were another continent and, if I'm honest, they still are a bit.

But even then, it wasn't all plain sailing and the opportunity to misbehave was never far away. Continuing the hospital theme, I have a lasting memory of going in for a knee operation in my early thirties and waking up in the recovery room covered by just a thin, green sheet. Next to me was an attractive woman sitting up with her hospital gown unintentionally open, and I have to admit to staring. Instantly, I'd built my own green tent that absolutely refused to go down – something to do with the effect of the anaesthetic, no doubt. Even as I was wheeled though the hospital corridors, desperately trying to think of something else, my little ridge tent was there for all to see. And then they took me in the lift with a bunch of strangers – at that point I could only hope I became invisible.

In my 40s and 50s, I'm not sure how I have felt about my relationship with my willy. We both like to reminisce sometimes, like old friends from university who get together occasionally to relive past adventures. I don't fully trust it, maybe because it can suddenly and with no warning decide not to work, or, worst of all, can lose interest half-way through. The bonds that held us together in earlier life have started to weaken and it is starting to show signs of being more of a problem than an asset.

So, what of the future? I have some hopes – apart from the avoidance of catheters and fingers up the bum. I'd like to grow old with great memories, even though we both know they are wildly exaggerated. I'd like to surprise both me and my wife by jumping on her sometimes, and, on a good day, stay awake until the end. I'd also like to have the occasional flirt with a well-preserved grandmother. And I'd like to keep my willy covered up, safe and warm, in the way you would an old pet who has been with you from the start. Its work will have been done.

Or maybe we should be more ambitious and channel Roger McGough, whose poem *Let Me Die A Youngman's Death*, first published in 1967, suggests some entertaining and adventurous ways to meet one's maker – at the age of 73, or 91, or maybe 104... And, until that day, let's rely on little blue tablets and a lack of self-awareness: the get-out-of-jail-free card that allows the occasional lapse into bad behaviour.

Malos Muchachos:
the Essence of a Boys' Trip

Travelling with like-minded mates, on what we euphemistically call boys' trips, gives some insight into the male psyche operating outside its normal habitat. It's something I've been doing most years over the last twenty-five, in a core group of three with many others who dip in and out. We have travelled all over the world, enjoyed a range of different activities and broadly employed the same jokes throughout. We have explored wildernesses in far-flung places, and been happy to camp on stony ground while washing in an ice river like the Yukon. Now, if possible, we prefer a bed and a shower at the end of a day doing silly things – and, if that can't be managed, I've researched the best possible lightweight camp beds, to avoid the necessity of lowering ourselves onto stony ground. In a desperate attempt to reverse the ageing process we haven't let up on the stuff we do, but now we do tend to go to bed by nine, in the sure and certain knowledge that we will be up three times in the night, and wake up more cranky than we did in our thirties. Recently, we were in Kyrgyzstan, riding truly crap bikes into a thirty-mile-an-hour headwind. It was over really rough and mountainous terrain, with no suspension and a saddle modelled on a house-brick. Dinner that night was a perfunctory affair, with half of us admitting that we had come close to quitting for the first time in all those years. So, we promised ourselves that we would go away, get properly fit and be ready and willing to battle through our sixties, just to be able to stay in the game. To be still going strong at seventy is the target.

The first key element of a boys' trip is being allowed to go, or, at least, allowing yourself to go. Our trips started as long weekends and have then stretched out to a week, then two weeks and sometimes two trips in a year – so it's been a slow, twenty-five-year process of acclimatisation for our families. In fairness, most of our partners have got used to the idea and seem to recognise that it's a necessary reboot of maleness. Some men duck out by blaming their wives, excuses which rarely stand up to scrutiny when you subsequently discover that their wives would have been delighted to get rid of them for a fortnight. Others sensibly consider that riding a house-brick downhill over boulders just might be a level of pain they can do without.

Fundamental to a successful trip has to be the activity, without which there would be no war stories to accompany dinner. We've done kayaking, canoeing, trekking, zip-wiring, abseiling, surfing, cycling and horse-riding, none of which seemed to require any meaningful competency on our part – or maybe they did in the brochure but we skipped over it. We have been chucked off horses, had a nose broken with a surfboard, capsized many times, failed to stop on a jungle zip-wire before hitting the platform and suffered real altitude sickness on mountain climbs – summed up by our riding guide in Chile who was so shocked by our incompetence that she still writes to us as 'Malos Muchachos' (English translation: bad boys).

Activities do two other key things – they make you so tired that you just don't care about anything and they provide God-given opportunities for stupidity. Tiredness is important because that feeling of achievement and fighting the odds is fundamental to blokedom. Doing dumb things feeds into an award system called 'Dick of the Day' – usually accompanied by a particularly ugly hat that has to be worn until there is another worthy recipient. Airport security is an especially good hunting ground for candidates, but really you need to be on your guard 24/7 if you don't want to be caught out. This seems to be very much a male thing and we have all developed highly sensitive antennae for the opportunities for ridicule. The ability to give and receive banter is a fundamental social skill for men, for good or bad, but it does need to follow certain rules: it must be funny, it mustn't be malicious and the intention should be good – but remember: you live by the sword, you die by the sword.

Women get discussed around the camp-fire, and pretty well anywhere else, and it's not decorous. As grown men, we'd hate to have the conversation recorded, but, once again, it's part of being a bloke – or, at least, we are led to believe it is part of being a bloke. Having said that, we are all talk and in all these years no one has come close to misbehaving – it's an idea best viewed from the outside and only in the abstract. We have never challenged each other to invite partners on our trips, which is fortunate, because I suspect they would a) be reluctant because they recognise the need for male bonding and b) hate them. I love mixed holidays but maybe both sexes need separation from time to time – it's liberating to be away in single-sex groups and probably helps the whole tribe to function thereafter.

The composition of the team is pretty important, though here men have an advantage over women in single-sex trips. If a man is being a complete dick, he will either be told to behave or just be ignored until he comes to his senses. A quick straw poll among my female friends and family suggests that women are much more likely to rally round the miscreant and get dragged into a search for meaning and reconciliation – blokes just won't do that, so sulking is a failed strategy from the start.

You do need a broad alignment of expectations, together with reasonably similar physical abilities. It's no good taking a city boy who is looking for a fine Merlot when the only thing available is fermented mares' milk. Also, you can't be the fat boy at the back all the time which, worryingly, is a role I'm starting to carve out for myself. I also recognise that it's good to have different skills and leadership qualities within the group, together with a willingness to follow when it's not your game. I may be the main organiser but, if I ever try to do something mechanical, I either get the job taken off me immediately, or I get ten or fifteen minutes of wry observation in the hope that I will get the 'Dick of the Day' award. Typically, someone is better at IT stuff and we have a few who enjoy cooking, so a lot of the contested areas are covered – it's a subtle model of leadership, and one we have developed by accident.

The beauty of any activity-based trip, for men or women, is the opportunity to put your mind into neutral. If you are trekking up a mountain, you have hours to think and discuss things with friends. It's a space we rarely give ourselves in our busy lives, but when you have none of the accoutrements of the modern world around, it liberates the mind. Burning thighs going up, gentle meandering coming down or the rolling gait of a horse, all in open countryside, provide space for us to concentrate on what is important. On these trips, businesses have been set up or reorganised, relationships reappraised and heads emptied of clutter – all despite the lack of material comfort. It would be wrong to paint a picture of men in floating robes, stroking pointy beards and philosophising for days on end – often the conversation doesn't get beyond morning bowel movements – but notwithstanding the variable nature of the discourse and subject matter, there is something very powerful in taking yourself into a neutral place, without the white noise of the everyday life.

Wilderness places are our particular shtick and the more remote the better. There is a price to pay for this, as travelling to them can be tortuous, with multiple flight connections and bumpy minibus journeys but, ultimately, they are worth the effort. If wild animals are involved, so much the better – encounters with snake eagles, bears and beluga whales are just some of the things that are seared into my memory.

In essence, boys' trips help strip away the layered pressures of society from the onion of male sociability and mental resilience. They are a curious mixture of humour, exhaustion, adventure, subtle competitiveness, space and fun: the chance for boys to be boys. I need to go back to the well of maleness and drink deeply at least once a year – and odd days scattered throughout the year help to keep me refreshed. They satisfy a primitive need and they also help me function in a multi-dimensional and, ultimately, more fulfilling society.

Hang On Snoopy, Snoopy Hang On!

Horse-riding in the wilderness of the Yukon is a fabulous experience, although somewhat perilous if you ride as badly as I do. I was given a horse called Snoopy and she was a bit special. She was predominantly white with irregular brown and black blobs, a wide girth and a cool, appraising look in her eye. It wouldn't be right to say we bonded, and it wasn't a relationship of equals, given her haughty nature, but we fell into a kind of easy, but barely tolerated, plodding rhythm. It was made clear to me very early on that cantering was not going to be an option, but there was sufficient excitement to be had, as she loved to walk close to the edge of sheer drops, and then throw in the odd theatrical stumble.

However, it was in the evening that Snoopy excelled. In remote country, it's quite important not to lose your horse, so we were instructed by the guide to tie them up carefully. My mate, Bob, did Snoopy for me, along with his horse, Hercules, so it was a little disconcerting to see only Hercules tied to the tree at breakfast. Bob fervently denied culpability but was sent off to find Snoopy, nonetheless. The next night I was very careful to tie her up, using our newly learned cowboy knot. Snoopy eyed it with indifference but that was just a ploy. Next morning – no Snoopy, although she did turn up at nosebag time. On the third night, I added an extra hitch, pulled it tight and spent a few minutes trying to reason with her. The next morning: no Snoopy, and no other horses either. She had undone her knots and then gone around all the others letting them off – just for kicks. They had found a lush green field, and we rounded them all up, but our guide had lost his patience. That night Snoopy was in the horse equivalent of a straitjacket and it worked. No more great escapes, but I can't help thinking she was a little diminished for the rest of the trip. In my eyes, she was a wonderfully maverick creature who was prepared to bide her time before delivering her *coup de grâce*. She knew perfectly well what she was doing. I felt that I been assessed, found wanting and given a lesson in how to execute a plan.

Drinking Culture and
the Culture of Drinking

Growing up in South Wales, we had our heroes, most notably three twenty-year-old blokes, who had achieved the dizzying feat of drinking four gallons of beer in a day. They started at nine in the morning and managed to put away thirty-two pints, including going home for dinner in the middle of it. I'm sure we had our other sporting or musical heroes but these guys were spoken of in hushed tones, having earned their own special corner of the White Rose.

I was tall enough to get my first pint in a pub served at fourteen and a half, and there began a drinking career that has stayed with me ever since – something, at the time, that was much more a male thing and reflects many of the masculine traits that continue to lead my sex astray. The purpose of going out became to drink as much as you could in a night, usually pints in double figures, but also to conform to the norms and behaviours that were expected of young men – we wanted to be accepted as part of the drinking gang, so we readily accepted the tribal rules. Maybe the more traditional male roles in South Wales had an influence, and certainly the rugby club mentality did, but drinking was the backbone of my lived experience for school, university and most of my twenties. I've taken pints into the urinal, just so I could keep up and not be the last to finish. I've stood on chairs in front of hundreds, necking a pint of Guinness and tomato juice, throwing it up into the same glass and then drinking it a second time – this seemed to buy me some serious credibility within the tribe. I've even done my own two-gallon challenge, managing a more modest sixteen pints, before walking out on friends, getting lost in a field of stinging nettles, setting off a fire alarm in another hall of residence, and somehow getting back to my room.

Then, of course, there are the drinking games and the culture attached to them. Inevitably, there is the alpha male in charge, and there are acolytes like the 'chief sneak' who watches for deviant behaviour and the 'generals' who are responsible for devising punishments. There are scores of different games; some of them involve mental agility, which is usually quickly impaired; others are just about drinking fast – like a boat race with two teams of eight downing pints in order, and being the first team to finish. Often there is fancy dress, or a uniform of sorts, differentiating the tribe from other drinking tribes, and, more insidiously, there are the subtle rules of the game that you have to understand to belong. If you don't know about the drinking left-handed rule or the different sequence of a game of Fizz-Buzz, then you are going to get punished more often. That can be just for fun, with no malice intended, but it's still a form of social control and compliance. Drinking is an admired skill in the young and, in a diluted version in adults, it is rewarded with social inclusion.

So why do some intelligent people drink to excess? Why do they spend vast amounts of money they can't afford, live with horrendous hangovers, piss off lovers, get into fights or sleep in doorways? And why does it go on across the country in seemingly time-honoured fashion?

Firstly, I think it's just fun, lubricated by the mind-altering drug that is alcohol. Being with friends, laughing and joking, is a really good part of being human, so let's not be too po-faced about it. We can relax more and maybe let the guard down by being silly and irresponsible – as an antidote to being the wage-earner, student or parent, who has to put on an act for large parts of our public lives. It's a kind of freewheeling, most of the time, though it probably helps to have some kind of stabilisers or regulator – without them, marriages can break down, laws can be broken and health can be seriously affected.

Next, there is the sense of belonging. We like to be close to others, to slap them on the back and share intimacies. As tribal animals, it's good to know the protocols and behaviours for being in the gang – because being in the gang is emotionally safe and meaningful. Not being in the gang can feel lonely and excluded. On the other hand, tribal behaviour can go too far and, even if the intentions are benign, sometimes, people can get hurt. Some don't have the tolerance for alcohol or will try too hard to play the game, going beyond normal limits. We've all had to get someone home who is in a mess or throwing up in the gutter – in fact most of us have been that person at some stage, because our common-sense regulators can go wonky.

Finally, there is the nice effect of alcohol itself. The first one or two drinks are great, and can give you the buzz you may be looking for. However, as a young man I have no memory of going out to experience a great tasting drink. I may have had a view on brands of lager or whiskey, but quantity not quality was the driver; quantity, and who you were sharing it with. Herein lies my salvation and my downfall. I can drink very quickly but I don't regulate the way a grown man should. After the first couple of drinks, I get only marginal pleasure before I pass into the 'too much' stage. That's because it's an addictive product which actively discourages intervention from our reason.

As I've got older, I have changed and improved, partly because I have the kind of responsibilities that encourage better behaviour, and partly because I can no longer handle alcohol in the way I used to. Yet I'm still the first to finish my drink, and still have alcohol-induced adventures that are embarrassing or inappropriate – the South Wales training never quite leaves you. My brain, though, has managed to get more of a handle on my lily-livered subconscious and I now have a much better relationship with drink. Over the years, I've tried many techniques to regulate it including: dry January; taking a week off every month; water in-between alcoholic drinks (terrible for a middle-aged bladder); restricting myself to only two types, for example, beer and wine but not spirits; only drinking at weekends; counting units in a week and many more strategies. Some of these worked, until I got bored with them and found myself obsessing about the end of my self-imposed restrictions. What does work and, of course, I should know this, is drinking more slowly and stopping after the buzz of the first couple. That is where the pleasure is and everything thereafter is marginal. The other trick is to distract myself at habitual drinking times, like before dinner – by playing tennis, working at the computer, phoning my parents, having a bath, or whatever.

I have had to force myself to answer the question about 'problem drinking'. It's an embarrassing question because it goes to the heart of 'am I in control here?' As men, my friends and I (and I know, because we've talked about it) want to feel we can control ourselves, but we also want the release that alcohol and company brings. It's the contradiction of allowing ourselves to relax from our normal, responsible behaviour, while submitting to the wholly different set of drinking rules that the tribe mandates. Maybe alcohol gives the release from the everyday challenges of life, without having to do the un-male thing of talking about what these challenges mean?

I think I've come to the conclusion that, while I might not be the master of alcohol, I'm not its dependent. I can stop for days and weeks, but I also recognise it as a pleasurable thing and I want it in my life – for social reasons and, as a sign of eventual maturity, because I can really enjoy the taste. It's also a mood enhancer that can give me a lift or calm me down – though there is still the devil on the shoulder that will try to give me the flimsiest of excuses to indulge. I just wish someone had been able to get some of this through to my younger self; certainly, my parents tried.

Having defined my master-and-servant relationship, I have to admit that the medical profession would use a very different yardstick. I was once asked, in a medical, how many units I drank in a week, and decided to answer honestly. I put down 'twenty-five' which was marked down as 'hazardous drinking' – so that's the last time I told the truth. I also notice that the sneaky bastards have cut men's safe levels to match women's, at fourteen units a week, and a unit is about a thimbleful. Best to ignore that particular leaflet in the doctor's waiting room.

Nowadays, I'll nurse a pint in the pub for much longer, while I observe younger people's drinking behaviour, albeit from the comfort of a seat in the corner rather than being jostled at the bar. That makes me sound very old and curmudgeonly, so I want to stress that I can stand at the bar, often for as much as twenty minutes, including two toilet breaks. The extraordinary thing is that the behaviour of the young almost exactly matches that of my generation – with the exception that today many more women and girls are involved in heavy drinking. There are the usual costumes or dress codes, the same drinking games, the equivalent social scrum and the typical in-group and out-group dynamics you'd expect. Boys' and girls' groups tend to be separate from each other at the start, but, as the evening progresses, you see the waters starting to mix. Then, of course, when someone is throwing up outside, girls will tend to help each other and be kinder, while boys will just laugh at the unfortunate miscreant.

The final dilemma is when you have teenage kids, who start to behave in similar ways. My daughter, not so much, though she has had her moments, but my son is exhibiting exactly the same tendencies I did. He's the first to finish a pint, plays all the games, lives with horrible hangovers and probably only tells me half of what he is up to. Hardly revelatory that kids don't tell their parents everything! A part of me is proud of him, in a blokeish kind of way, but there is a bigger part of me that worries about both the short- and long-term effects. Short-term, because boys can get hurt or into trouble through drinking too much, and long-term because patterns can be established that are hard to break away from. At my age, I can still reference my teenage habits as I look mournfully at my empty glass – when everyone else in the round is only halfway through theirs.

I will hold onto the memories of smoky bars with sticky carpets, laughing uncontrollably with friends, singing tunelessly to Robbie Williams and that first gulp of a pint when you've really deserved it and all is well with the world. Plus, I expect to make many more memories that don't include throwing up in gutters. I hope my kids, and young people in general, enjoy drinking and socialising as it's such a fun part of life. Maybe they will learn to control it better and, as a result, enjoy it even more. I'm reconciled to the fact that drink is an important part of my life; it's my escape from the constant noise in my head and I don't see much wrong with that. It's exhausting always to have to be in control, and alcohol is an acceptable drug that gives me a break from being me.

Transitioning

I'm in a strange place, having decided, probably, not to work again full-time, and wondering what I'm going to do with the rest of my life. On top of this, we are living in the shadow of the pandemic, which suspended so many people's plans, and changed the world as we knew it into something only half-recognisable. The full effect will not fully emerge for years but there are clearly psychological and practical implications affecting everyone. I also know that I'm very lucky, being reasonably financially secure, and having escaped the more tragic consequences of Covid-19. I should see my transition as a high-quality problem, but like most of my species, when I try to put my problems in context I normally fail – we humans are just too invested in our own issues. So, I want to explore the process of transition out of work as I can't believe I'm alone in struggling through it, though it's clear there are many different coping strategies.

The first thing to highlight is the changing nature of status, especially between the employed and the retired. Hopefully we are not talking about the ego-driven, chest-thumping idea of status that some people protect, though most of us will have some residual memories and experience of that. One of the first questions we ask of strangers and friends, and are asked in turn, is

'What do you do?' or 'What are you doing these days?' and it can feel like a terrifying chasm not to have a clear answer – the answer that being employed always effortlessly furnished. However irrational it may be, especially as most have contributed through life, it's still difficult if there is no label to present. Many qualify it with 'retired, but spending time with grandchildren' or 'retired, but with so many jobs around the house, I wonder how I found the time to work,' or 'retired, but doing all sorts of bits and pieces'. It's a brave person who says 'I'm retired – now would you like to understand the emotional, intellectual and historical complexity that makes me worth talking to?' I hope this gets easier over time but it's a part of a change most of us have to go through.

Also, work is social, providing important mental and emotional challenges. I fully accept that I have been fortunate in broadly enjoying my career, and that some people just hate work and want to stop, but it's a loss I feel keenly. I could spend most days meeting friends or at the baker's, talking to others in the queue, but it doesn't replace the problem-solving and community dynamics that work provides – even if it's as simple as word-smithing in a document, brainstorming an issue or just gossiping about who is doing what to whom. It's this dynamic, that plays to my need to belong, that will drag me back to some form of work, or hopefully some form of voluntary activity.

Or maybe it's the timing that is wrong – do people finish work too soon or, in some cases, hang on in work too long? Optimum timing will depend on the individual and their circumstances – and there may not be a free choice – but it's something that needs careful consideration. I worked with a lovely gentleman (in the positively old-fashioned sense of the word) in a high-intensity production planning role, who was finally forced to give up work.

He went from one hundred miles an hour to a complete standstill, and was dead within six months. This is not an unheard-of scenario and it should worry us, both as individuals and society. It wastes productive talent that could be doing something fulfilling, and gives too much power to work as a way of giving meaning to life.

Then there is the body, which simply can no longer do all you want it to do. Somehow, this seems more obvious when you don't have to go into an office or factory – driving, walking, sitting in meetings. Now you have the time to play golf, take the mountain bike out with friends, play tennis or walk the dog uphill and down dale. Then you find that the game of tennis yesterday means you walk like you've got a broomstick up your bum for golf the next day, and you need a hot bath in order just to be able to empty the dishwasher. It's one of life's great ironies that, when your body is at its best, you are working or parenting so much that you don't have time to enjoy it. Then when you have more than enough time, your body looks at you and says, 'Really? You're having a laugh.' No amount of yoga or muesli will reverse the ageing process, and the best you can hope for is to slow or ease the decline.

There is a good chance that suddenly being at home for seven days a week will prove to be a major obstacle to domestic harmony. Maybe you live alone; maybe you are home alone, while your partner is still working; or maybe you are just in the way when your partner has a well-established routine. You could also have to spend an awful lot more time with a partner and find that you don't have so much to say to one another; or that you need to reframe a relationship that may have involved thirty years of completely different levels of engagement. Then there are domestic chores. Do you need to share the work out differently, and how does that work if one partner has developed systems and competencies that the newbie has to learn – and gets wrong? Jokingly, I suggested a ten-year tapering for the sharing of responsibilities after leaving work, but this went down badly.

One of the key learnings is that we have different levels of change at different times of our lives and they need to be treated differently. It may be the birth and caring for children, the death of a loved one, health problems or sudden unemployment, but it will be a shock. If we plot our lives with intensity/stress on the vertical axis and time on the horizontal axis, most of us will have experienced spikes on top of the everyday shape – good and bad. If we are lucky, we have friends and family to help us through, though we have to recognise that these same people may also be going through their own separate, or related, transitions.

For most people in late middle age, the challenges of parenting have shifted. We probably don't need to stop our offspring sticking their fingers in plug sockets anymore, but we will have concerns regarding just about every aspect of their lives: their learning, their employment, and their dodgy partners. While we had authority at the plug socket stage, now they have their own agency and 'do as you're told' is a poor strategy. In short, the worries and feelings of responsibility remain the same, but the power to do anything about them disappears. It's the way of the world, but it does tend to leave the parent with a very different job that they are not fully prepared for. No more driving to football matches or holding hands as they cross the road – they drive themselves to football and just try grabbing their hand at a zebra crossing now! I'm sure they won't give the old man's loss a second thought, but it's another transition on top of a bunch of other changes.

I've turned into the Ancient Mariner, in that I keep stopping one in three men, to ask them about their experience of transitioning.

It's fair to say that many look at me as if I'm smoking something, because, of course, they wanted to stop work and enjoy a long and easy-going retirement. Many of these are practical people, who happily want to build that shed, or strip down the engine of an old MGB. But, in that arena, I'm one of the most useless men you will ever meet – my wife brought the electric drill to our relationship, and the only tool I can operate with any competence is a credit card. Helping with grandchildren gives life purpose for many men I speak to, while there are plenty, including me, who want to travel more. Finally, there is another group with whom I can equally identify, who still have that need to be doing something externally. We are still searching for meaning and the recognition that something useful is going on. We will then feel good about the contribution we are making, though I suspect we are not terribly easy to live with while we are working this out.

Pulling all this together, I'm starting to appreciate how this particular period of transition is pretty major and, learning from other significant inflection points in life, I can see how it could have profound mental health implications for people in my cohort – that group of middle- and late-middle-aged blokes who can still successfully breathe on a mirror. Without a professional role, we can lose the external signifiers of value, as well as the inner-life assurance that we have a purpose. Finally, our bodies are giving us the 'gypsy's warning' that we are not immortal and, reluctantly, we are going to have to accept that rest days may have to be built into the schedule. And, of course, it can be any combination of all of the above – different for different people and different circumstances, but still a fact of life.

There are solutions that can mitigate against the mental health and happiness issues for those affected. Recognising that it is really important and, therefore, thinking it through, long before the event, can only help. I acknowledge that talking is easier for some men than for others, but I remain convinced that it will help most of us if we address this transition with sensitivity. Ideally, we'd start talking early in the process but timing is not always under our control, and anyway it's rarely a one-off conversation. Discussing these matters with loved ones and trusted friends can be very powerful, even if you hear yourself saying the blindingly obvious. Talking things through, and discovering that others have experienced similar feelings, can be very reassuring and contribute to good mental health hygiene.

If you are uncomfortable with sharing your feelings with loved ones, who may be part of the problem, a good doctor can refer you to other 'talking' or 'chemical' solutions. At the risk of generalisation, I suspect that men are less well equipped to face this life change and are more impacted by it – and, as is well documented, our gender is pretty crap at talking about our emotions and problems.

Society and employers can have a material role in protecting individuals – with education and imaginative support options. A friend at Mercedes was encouraged to wind down his days per week over a two-year period, thereby helping him in the transition process and keeping his expertise in the business for longer. He is now happily running a B&B in Northumbria, while Mercedes rewarded and transferred the knowledge of a valued employee.

A large number of people crave, embrace and enjoy retirement, so for many it will not be a disruptive process. But for those who may not be taking it quite so well, a few open questions, a phone call and the offer of a beer might just help.

Giving Ourselves a Sporting Chance

Sport is to masculinity as gravy is to meat – a natural pairing that complements, enhances and gives texture to each. It provides one of the central ways in which men relate to each other, whether or not they are sports fans. Even if a man has the courage to confess a complete lack of interest in sport, his stance requires an explanation – in a way that a coolness towards music, the arts or beekeeping doesn't. This is clearly not to ignore brilliant, focused and passionate women who play or watch sport, but it just doesn't appear to be so central to understanding the collective female psyche. Most men will have had defining moments in sport, whether it's scoring the winning runs at under-elevens or coming in last and miserable from a school cross-country run.

Sporting loyalties are a constant currency of man-to-man communication. It's almost guaranteed that, in most social or work settings, you will eventually be asked what team you support – and the answer 'I don't' runs the risk of being something of a conversation killer. Some men fly under a flag of convenience and latch onto sport just to have something to say, though that's a high-risk strategy. If, like former Prime Minister David Cameron, you exhort your audience to support West Ham, having frequently declared your undying loyalty to Aston Villa, you will be found out.

If you are not a real sports fan, it's better to discuss beekeeping or Pre-Raphaelite painting as a more authentic alternative, even if it might not find so many easy alliances.

Sport has many roles in society, evidencing fabulous variety at all levels of ability. It enriches us because of its outward expressions – we can participate or engage with other like-minded people – and its psychological healing – sport can connect directly with some of our most profound individual needs.

Most people have a degree of competitiveness in them. It can be a desire to beat the other guy or team, but it can also manifest as the need of the individual to be the best they can be. Sport can satisfy both these needs. A Manchester football derby, for example, will ignite the passion of the players and supporters, harnessing the waves of human emotions that make them feel alive. Or I can compete with myself and, while I will probably only ever fluke a penalty against an international goalkeeper, I can still try to be the best penalty-taker I can be. Sport is about testing ourselves, externally and internally, while grabbing hold of our end of the emotional see-saw. The downs can be upsetting and the ups can give a false euphoria, but that is part of the deal when we engage in sport at any level.

My gender can also produce the borderline psychotics in sport, like cyclist Lance Armstrong or 'Mad John', a flanker from Waunarlwydd who beat seven bells out of me playing rugby against my village team. These people are probably at the extremities of behaviour, but I'm convinced they are more of a male thing, with very few women displaying the 'wild eyed scariness' that ultra-competitive men do – although ice skater Tonya Harding, who allegedly arranged for a competitor to be beaten up, is probably made more of 'puppy dog tails' than 'sugar and spice'. Sport combines skill and competitiveness and, from observation, men and women can generally exhibit both – but it is competitiveness's darker cousin, aggression, where some of the more troubling differences lie. The male sex is generally the most aggressive, for evolutionary and psychological reasons, and sport can reflect this. Additionally, this propensity for aggression can be stirred up by an audience baying for blood, and then passion and competitiveness get replaced by something altogether more damaging.

At a primitive level, sport can be seen as a substitute for hunting. We no longer have to go in search of woolly mammoths but we do have the need to bend our minds and bodies to winning or achieving something. When we are playing sport, whether we are on the pitch at Lord's or on the village bowling green, we are out there in the savannah and we are competing. Very few of us provide wildebeest carcasses for the table anymore, but sport allows us to use our bodies in ways that the bodies of our caveman ancestors were designed for. Sporting success can also be conflated with other primitive social needs, including sex, where the pursuit of sporting glory allows contemporary man to show off his physical prowess. As the successful hunter has more chance of mating, so, probably, does the successful sportsman. Bringing home meat or shiny medals seem to be evolution's way of 'getting the girl'. This was brilliantly illustrated by the England centre forward, Peter Crouch, who was unlikely to have a fallback career as a male model. When asked what he would have been if he wasn't a professional footballer, he answered, 'A virgin'.

Sport is social and fulfils that most basic of human needs: the desire to connect. In the crowd or on the pitch, we want to connect with our fellow man, especially if we are about to get hot and sweaty. Clearly, there are individual activities like running and cycling, but the proliferation of park runs or cycling clubs seems to show that we still need the extra dimension of collective endeavour. 'Social' can, however, be stretched to a more sinister iteration of 'tribal', where we celebrate the success of our tribe at the expense of another – overriding the more collective benefits of 'being in the gang'. The disappointment of the losing tribe amplifies our own feeling of happiness when we win. Winning is not always enough in its own right, so we want to double up on the euphoria by enjoying another tribe's misery – similar to the psychology of comedy when we can enjoy both the joke and someone else's misfortune. The most extreme expression of this sporting rivalry is when we demonise the opposition in a way that embeds hate and emphasises exclusion. Capitalising on the failure of others accentuates both the negative and the positive responses, adding up to a psychological rush – but it's a strong and dangerous drug. Anyone watching groups of men in a football crowd will wonder how rational, grown-up, family guys can turn into bug-eyed, bulging-necked lunatics when spotting another tribe in different shirts.

Sport can also be used for political gain on the international stage, captured by the new term 'sports-washing' – where countries seek to distract from human rights abuses or political oppression by using major sporting events to gain legitimacy and influence on the world stage. The most famous example is the Berlin Olympics in 1936 when Hitler looked to promote the racial superiority of the Aryan race – only to have his plan beautifully undermined by the Black athlete, Jesse Owens, who won four gold medals. Other examples include the boycott of the 1980's Moscow Olympics, the sporting isolation of the South African apartheid regime and the human rights abuses highlighted by the 2022 Qatar World Cup

– all representing some of the most important moral dilemmas woven into the commercialisation of sport.

Finally, sport or competitive activity can be appreciated just for the joy of moving – the buzz of making our muscles and minds work to achieve something. While reading the Sunday papers in bed rewards day-to-day striving, it isn't what our bodies were made for. My young son used to run, jump and twist in the air just for the sheer pleasure of it, but as grown-ups we are too sophisticated or embarrassed to do that – sport gives us the excuse.

There are so many types of sport that it's a fool's game to try and define it, except to say that it does seem to fit on a spectrum from gladiatorial to pure team endeavour – gladiatorial in a *mano a mano* way, like tennis or fencing, or team-led, like football or hockey when, broadly, you play for the greater good – and all points in-between. Cricket is obviously a team game but it is the individual battles that define success, as you face down a man trying to take your head off with a hard lump of cork in a leather casing. Rugby is a team sport but includes the lonely role of goal-kicker – and who, but the extraordinarily mentally disciplined, would want to take a penalty for the team in a world cup shootout?

Winning as part of a team can also be a high, inspiring such collective joy that many of us are happy to weave our own feelings into the tapestry of the team's narrative. The trick, for the individual, is to recognise what best suits their character and what gives the most satisfaction. I know I would be a gibbering idiot walking up to take that critical penalty but some of my life's best moments have been hugging other sweaty blokes as the team did something extraordinary. Of course, we can all flit along the spectrum as much as we like, but understanding our sporting psychology is useful if we want to get the most out of one of the best human experiences. It helps us understand masculinity because it is woven into society, and specifically the society of men; whether we are interested or not, it's very hard to ignore. While sport has its negatives, it also has massive physiological, psychological and social benefits – especially for the half of the population that isn't in the first team for talking about feelings.

Sport been an incredibly important part of my life, especially as I moved around the country for different jobs. Sport gave me a social life when I was lonely and somewhere to go on training nights and match days. It gave me community and excitement, disappointment and elation – in short, emotional and physical succour. It kept me fit and moving, though I am now reliant on advances in medical science to correct the battering my body has taken. Sport gave me a narrative, in that I was a rugby or tennis player, and therefore it helped me find my tribe. Finally, there were mental health benefits that I'm only now starting to fully appreciate. Sport satisfied the social and primitive needs for sure, but there were deeper needs around self-esteem and taking a break from living in my own head. It offered an escape valve when the world and the 'self' got too much. There have been a few 'black dog days' in my life, but exercise and sport have always helped me re-establish and ground myself in the here and now. Ironically, even if I've played badly, and could beat myself up for it, there is still the overall positive effect of just getting out there and doing stuff. During one particular period, I guess I'd be defined as depressed, and I was certainly lost. I signed up for external help. The therapist was really useful in connecting the dots of my past and future challenges, but there was a key piece of advice that has stuck with me. If you are feeling down, go out and make yourself absolutely exhausted – not just a half hour run but two hours' worth of exercise, ideally outside. It helps you sleep; you feel you are achieving something and you can put your mind into neutral – giving you a rest from your own brain. Simply put, it's hard to be sad when you are out of breath.

Age and sport are strange bedfellows and I oscillate between deep frustration and happy resignation that I'm still in the game. For most of my life, I have been a reasonably good sportsman, though never the fastest or the fittest. I relied on good hand-to-eye coordination, what were strangely called strong 'twitch' muscles, and being a good team player. I also had a will to win which probably meant I won more than I lost when playing against my contemporaries. This worked well into my forties, as I frantically exercised in a forlorn attempt to reverse the ageing process. I became an impulse shopper for neoprene bandages and had a physio on speed dial in case I needed a fix of ultrasound. By this time, I'd lost all my own front teeth, had had three operations on one knee and was only able to move thanks to plenty of Vaseline and Sloane's Liniment. I'd wisely chosen playmates who were of similar ages and states of repair to me, and we entered into a Faustian pact to pretend we were still young men.

But then the inevitable happened: my playmates started to give up, and my body started to give up on me. I now only had younger guys to play against if I wanted to carry on or a couple of older ones who had wisely concentrated on non-impact sports like cycling. Old injuries stopped repairing themselves, my lungs would burn minutes after starting and I needed two days in between each escapade to recover. Fortunately, we had moved into a bungalow by this stage, so I didn't have the indignity of having to come down the stairs backwards each morning.

Most troubling of all is how my reactions have slowed down

dramatically and my ever-reliable hand-to-eye coordination has started to desert me. Playing tennis recently, I found myself at the net... my partner served... my brain told me that the other guy was going to pass me down the line and then... 'how the fuck did the ball get behind me?' This happens more and more now and seems to worsen with age for both sexes. It's called proprioception and it's essentially the reduced ability to understand where your body and limbs are in space – or, colloquially, 'the silly old bastard has lost it'.

The other thing to contend with is that now, unexpectedly, I don't care so much if I win or lose. Sure, I care about playing to the best of my ability, but the fire has started to go out. This feels like a threat to my masculinity, because aren't we supposed to want to win at all costs? Aren't we supposed to be ready to leap to the defence of loved ones or be fast and skilled enough to catch lunch? Or am I over-thinking this and all that happened is I just lost a game of tennis?

What is clear is that sport and ageing reflect on each other, both physically and psychologically – and then the whole thing gets wrapped up in our self-esteem. It's something we just have to find ways of compensating for, but there are ways. Stretching and clumsy 'bloke yoga' really do work and are a lot less harmful than a half-hour run. They bore me to tears but there again so does the run – it's the price we pay to stay on the pitch, court or in the saddle. A couple of days off exercise each week also works, as our bodies need to recover – plus we can trick our bodies by alternating different sports which use different muscles. I'm teetering on the edge of getting an electric mountain bike, although, were it not for the legitimacy given by mates, I'd probably feel it was putting one foot in the grave. I walk now rather than run, but if I can include enough hills, I can burn off the same energy, though it takes longer. I play doubles rather than singles now, as throwing up on the side of the court is not a good look – plus I try to choose a younger partner and designate them as the team runner.

Sport and its stable-mate exercise give us so much, physically, and they also deliver social benefits, mental health improvements and genuine life experiences. They are rightly a key part of most curricula. We get to use our bodies and minds as they are designed to be used, and, internationally, we compete on the pitch and the track, hopefully, rather than going to war. Clearly, sport is only one element of our social interactions but it is part of the psyche of being human. It is integral to most societies in one form or another and it gives us powerful insights into how we can, and do, behave as social animals.

I'll finish with a description of a sport I witnessed in Kyrgyzstan. Two village teams turned up on horseback to a flat piece of land with makeshift goals about half a kilometre apart. A goat was beheaded and then the aim was to pass the carcass between team members at ludicrous speed, grabbing the animal's leg and using a swinging motion to facilitate various intricate moves, while the opponents tried to knock you off your horse, and gain possession of the goat – in a game somewhat akin to polo. The game lasted about an hour, until the goat disintegrated. One team won and village pride was enhanced, while the other team resolved to do better next time – then, exhausted and sweaty, they all went off to get pissed on foul-tasting, fermented mare's milk. I imagine the most successful goat swinger then got to invite the prettiest girl back to his yurt and, as commentators often say, 'sport was the winner' – unless, of course, you take the goat's perspective.

Fathers and Sons

As a seventeen-year-old, I read Turgenev's *Fathers and Sons*, along with other Russian classics, because I thought it would impress girls and get me laid. It did neither of these things. What it did do was to bury itself deep in my subconscious and eventually emerge to provoke the question of relationships through the generations, especially reflecting on changing ideas about masculinity.

I recently had the pleasure of sitting down and discussing this with my ninety-one-year-old father and twenty-one-year-old son. We explored the work environment, living in a modern world and, inevitably, how men react to and treat women. The conversation also strayed into topics such as how we manage our emotions and our fears.

My dad did National Service and still advocates the benefits of army discipline for society, despite the certain knowledge that his son would be truly terrible at taking orders. Dad was demobbed into a bowler-hatted, suit-wearing world where men's jobs had a career path and women's jobs, in the typing pool or admin departments, were expected to end with the arrival of children. Men felt protective towards women, though my father was honest enough to say how they terrified him and his mates. He used the phrase 'as fragile as Dresden glass', at the same time as recalling how powerful and frightening women could be. As a matter of principle, he would always give up his seat on the tube to a woman, but still has the scars of rejection when he had to walk across an empty floor to ask a girl to dance.

The overarching question of how he managed his emotions, fears and concerns was met with a few seconds of incredulity, almost as if he hadn't thought much about it before. In my dad's world, you just 'got on with it'. You might discuss practical things with your wife but even those discussions probably didn't touch much on feelings. 'Chivalrous' was my son's word for it, embodying courtesy, taking responsibility and putting up with the shit even if you didn't cause it.

I love my dad very much, but up until my late teens he was more of a shadowy figure who went to work and was the last line of defence when I had finally driven my mother to distraction: a typical male role at the time. He was fair and reasonable but we didn't have the depth of emotional experience and history that softened any conflict. My siblings and I developed an ability to negotiate conflict with our mother, because it was an everyday thing, but the male disciplinary role of supporting the other parent made arguing with him seem more serious. I do remember him making a big mistake once, by supporting my argument when I'd stormed out of the house in a hissy fit – I was quickly forgiven but my mother didn't speak to him for nearly a week.

When I was growing up, in the seventies and eighties, the established model of behaviour – 'protect and provide' – began to give way to more outward displays of maleness. We dressed and acted tough, and had the confidence of the young, but we had also been handed the loaded gun of masculinity – without any training on how to use it or the life experience to understand it. No doubt, the age difference previously afforded by National Service had an impact, as it had given a couple more years of maturity to earlier generations. My peer group benefited from the invention of teenagers in the late fifties and sixties, so went full on for drinking, doing dumb things and treating women as sexual challenges. I'm sure my dad's generation did some of these things, but they had been through the Second World War and subsequent austerity, and probably had fewer opportunities to be badly behaved.

Later, when my generation transitioned to the world of work or university, we carried on with these attitudes, albeit with the creeping realisation that women were not the soft touches we had originally thought. Women were academically more mature and now both genders were encouraged to commit to a career path. Massive inequality still existed, especially around pay, but having abandoned our part as protectors and providers, men were left with no apparent positive role on the social stage. We needed to assert some kind of identity and we generally went for the shallow, outward demonstrations of masculinity. As young men, we tried to be self-confident, assertive and competitive, despite being scared boys just below the surface. We didn't talk about feelings but worked on the principle that if everyone else seemed happy, there must be something in this masculine malarkey.

I would say that my son's generation is not as clumsy about masculinity as we were, though they still have to handle the complexity of entry into a society of men and women. It appears that traits like integrity, authenticity, self-awareness and care for or appreciation of others are pushing through against the old characteristics of physical strength and assertiveness. A subtle addition from my son was masculine strength as demonstrated by 'the guy you listen to when he speaks'.

The concept of protection is still there in modern masculinity but it's so much more nuanced. This generation of men is still unlikely to let a girl walk home on her own at night, but may have to couch it in terms of 'I was going your way anyway'. This softening of masculinity has been driven by increasing societal awareness, with better education for both sexes, and by a more flexible understanding of the role of women. We may have not completely crossed the Rubicon in terms of equality between the sexes, but the balance of power seems to be shifting, at least provisionally, and men are adapting to it.

In one way, it is more challenging because young men are now having to compete within a wider, globalised pool for jobs and resources, while society at home is encouraging positive discrimination in favour of women and disadvantaged groups. I make no comment on the rights and wrongs of this which is an essay for another book, but it's part of the mix forcing men to adapt. On top of structural changes in masculinity and femininity, everyone in my son's generation is bombarded with superficial images, messages and pressure to conform to sexual stereotypes. While these influences were always there in previous generations, the reach of social media means that they are now almost unavoidable. It must be hugely confusing. It's a headwind against enlightened masculinity and, more importantly, it drives unhappiness and mental health problems as young people strive to achieve the unachievable. In spite of that, we are starting to see the emergence of male role models who combine the competitive with the sensitive, like David Beckham or Tyson Fury. What is also encouraging is this generation's willingness to talk amongst friends about emotions and feelings, which is a good start.

If you add sex and sexual attraction into the equation, it starts to get really messy. It's not something I like to think too much about, but I strongly suspect that sex had a role in my arrival on this planet. Human beings fancy each other, and we are attracted by qualities that often reflect accepted masculine and feminine mores – whether we are heterosexual or have other orientations. Characteristics of masculinity and femininity are the currency by which we enter the mating game. If men believe that traditional or modern manifestations of masculinity improve their chances of 'getting the girl', they will accentuate these traits. We might get lucky or maybe we will have to do the walk of shame back across an empty dance floor.

At a basic level, some of the challenges for my dad, me and my son are the same, though the environment around us keeps altering. We have biology and sexual attraction baked into us, while changes in our world make us adapt and compromise. I consider myself to be very lucky to have come from parents who instinctively believed in and practised equality of the sexes, while accepting that both brought different things to the relationship. I'd also heartily recommend having sisters – my dad didn't, while my son and I have, so for us, girls are marginally less frightening and less shrouded in mystery. Good masculinity can flow through the generations and I suspect the same is true for more aggressive masculinity. It's moved from the chivalrous, through outward and shallow displays, to a highly nuanced balance of equality and awareness of gender differences.

I've been a son and a father and I'd reflect on the frustration and nonsense that is our inability to learn life lessons from our parents. Boys are programmed to make the same mistakes as we did, as they break away from the family, and all we can do is stand and watch, or, maybe, subtly influence if we have the patience of

Gandhi. I did it; my son will do the same and so will his sons, so the best we can do is be the safety net when things go wrong.

In *Fathers and Sons*, Turgenev explored this breaking away of sons from their parents, and the need to create new identities, so this is nothing new. I'm not worried about any nihilist tendencies in my son; I just wish he didn't leave his pants in the hallway.

Men and the Patriarchy

The sad truth is that men, throughout history, have behaved very badly indeed in relation to women and girls. In his excellent book *A History of Masculinity*, Ivan Jablonka comprehensively catalogues man's establishment, exercise and abuse of power down the centuries. He draws interesting and nuanced conclusions, but most powerfully and simply his verdict is we behaved that way 'because we could'. We could exploit our physical strength, we could use our natural assertiveness and competitiveness and we could take risks to have our own way. We also didn't have the inconvenience of childbirth and nurturing, so could concentrate more on attending to our selfish needs.

The patriarchy, as it has come to be called, promoted the role of men and then co-opted the rest of mankind to circle the wagons. It is a system of beliefs and values that is embedded in our political, economic and social institutions and is designed to advantage the interests of men. Worse still, it has tended to overlay white, wealthy, racist and religiously intolerant attitudes to establish the wheels-within-wheels that deliver power in society. I wonder whether women have ever wanted this power for its own sake, or are concerned with fairness and equality of opportunity, rather than hegemony. However, some forms of power will always play more to male biology and traits, giving us the advantage and the tools to succeed. The sexes were competing for different territory and, certainly through most of history, there was only one winner.

'The patriarchy' is a loaded phrase, often combined with 'masculine hegemony', and extended into 'toxic masculinity'. All these phrases, in one way or another, represent the male abuse of women and girls – and men can stand in the dock for the first two. However, where I part company is the use and promotion of the phrase 'toxic masculinity'. If masculine is what we are, deep within our being, then to tell half the population that they are fundamentally bad or toxic is very wrong. While it may not be a blanket comment on all men, if it becomes a fixed idea in the minds of men, especially young men, it will be hugely dangerous. It undermines self-worth in a world where insecurities and loneliness are endemic. It implies that women can do no wrong and men just can't help themselves doing wrong things, neither of which is true, though the scales are unevenly weighted. I would also challenge the view that in order to create a better world you only need to bring men and boys up better, by controlling their destructive impulses. This ignores positive male characteristics and is potentially unfair and isolating. We should criticise and call out toxic behaviours but not ascribe the word to the essence of someone's being, just because they are part of a group.

At the extremes of the toxic masculinity debate, we may get the wrong reactions, such as those of the 'incel' (involuntary celibate) movement with its aggression toward women, or maybe we will get men just disengaging from the debate – feeling the die is already cast against them. More insidious is the impact upon men's mental health: among fifteen- to twenty-nine-year-old men, suicide is the biggest cause of death, with a three to one ratio compared to young women. It's an age when men are trying to understand themselves in a frighteningly fast-changing world – and then society tells them that they may well just be 'rotten to the core'. Finally, it should be recognised that many male qualities are good for society even if they have contributed to a patriarchal history. Risk-taking in protecting others and pushing the boundaries of how we live are good qualities. The role of the provider underpins our safety and wellbeing, while competitive natures can improve or change society. A lot of male qualities can be found in the female sex as well and it's not helpful to attribute certain traits exclusively to one group. We need each other, hopefully for something more than just procreation. Then, overlaying all this, we also have to recognise that some, or many, alpha male characteristics are sexually attractive to women, which becomes a perpetuating story – as if it wasn't complicated enough! I remember a cartoon that stuck in my mind as a young man – a scrawny guy, tied to a post at Greenham Common, with one of the women saying to a journalist, 'Oh, him! We only keep him for breeding purposes'.

I will not defend the indefensible and the impact of the patriarchy has, throughout history, often been unacceptable – fuelled by masculine traits and behaviours. However, I hope the world is moving on, certainly in liberal democracies, though the 2022 reversal of US abortion laws should be a warning signal against complacency. Technology, contraception, changes in work and education have had a big role, as have fearless campaigners from the feminist and civil rights movements. I hope and believe that the opportunities for exploitation have been diminished, and that we are moving towards a fairer, more equal society. If there is a person-shaped hole out there, anyone should be able to fit into it. Of course, we must be wary of back-sliding, and the danger is not over, but we do need to recognise the importance of good relationships between men and women: relationships that can be playful, supportive, cooperative, respectful and open. My personal belief is that they are the best way to bring up children and, in any partnership, we should provide each other with emotional and physical succour as we navigate this crazy world. Understanding masculinity, in all its forms, is an inescapable part of this.

Why do my Glasses keep going Off-Grid?

I'm at the stage in life when glasses have moved from a tolerated intrusion to a necessary encumbrance if I want to function in the world. I have two proper, optician-prescribed pairs that I've tried to organise, but as soon as I've got one pair pinned down, the other goes walkabout. It won't be found in any of its designated places and it will not materialise until I've lost the first pair. Then it will turn up in an old coat pocket, underwater at the bottom of my hot-tub or, bizarrely, in the fridge. It's as if the two pairs operate a kind of magnetic pole effect that means they can't be in the same room together. I know which is which because one pair has lost the nice soft bits that stop you viciously scarring the bridge of your nose, while the others are so scratched that I can barely see through them. I suspect I'll have to go to the optician's again but I'll need two appointments, given the glasses' reluctance to play nicely together.

Of course, there are coping strategies, mainly based around lots of cheap pairs that can be left in designated places. I have to leave a 'wise owl' pair by my bikes or I won't be able undo the padlocks or see the pump dial. There's a pair in the kitchen, otherwise I can't read any packaging or cooking instructions – but they are in cahoots with the prescription ones and have a cloak of invisibility. In my car's glovebox, there is a pair that I rashly bought from garden centre. They are large, green and flowery, so I look like a Miss Huggit, who always asks a question on *Gardeners' Question Time*, and is honorary president of the Staines and Datchet Horticultural Society. Please don't judge me – I was desperate when I bought them. The final piece in the set is my old faithful pair in the bedside table drawer. They are probably a grade 1, although I'm currently moving up and away from a grade 2.5. They also only have one arm, but as long as there are no sudden movements, they kind of work. Clearly things have got desperate, but I have stopped short of wearing glasses on a chain around my neck, like a 1970s drag queen – because if I do my wife has threatened never to have sex with me again.

Anyone got any suggestions? About the glasses, not the sex.

The Tyranny of the Bow

Putting on my walking boots today, it struck me how useless, but all-pervasive, the bow is in our lives. The ability to tie a bow before you go to school has always been a rite of passage; otherwise, presumably, you'd lose your shoe and, before a responsible adult spotted it, you'd have lost a foot.

Having mastered the skill, we all endure lace-ups of some kind for the rest of our lives, until we are so old that, when they have been tied, we cannot return to the vertical without assistance. The veteran American comedian Jack Benny famously said that when he tied his laces, he tried to think of something else to do while he was down there.

My central argument is that bows are nothing more than shit knots. However tightly you tie them, they slowly work their way free over a couple of hours, because they are no match for the friction caused by feet that move up and down – which is what feet are designed to do – and so they need constant retying. The alternative is to risk tripping over your undone laces and falling under the bus, or to do a double knot, which negates the whole point of a bow. Its raison d'être is to operate as a quick release knot, and if it doesn't fulfil that fundamental function, you might as well tie a reef knot. The problem, of course, is that slip-ons are useless for playing football in, and Velcro is for those who missed the first day of infant school 'tie a bow' deadline.

The best reason I can see for persevering with bows is that they look like cute bunny ears flopping around. Essentially, though, bows in your laces are failed knots with great PR, and it's time someone called them out for the tyrants that they are.

IT and Me

I came to IT relatively late in life and it's never been an easy relationship. In truth, what I'm really hoping for is a *Day of the Triffids*-type event where the internet crashes and the calls go out:

'Is the analogue man out there?'

'Does someone still know how to read a map or has anyone got the capability to remember around ten telephone numbers of family and close friends?'

'Experience of using a fax machine would be useful, as would knowledge of how to put real coins in a parking meter.'

In my mind, my time will have come and I'll be carried shoulder-high down the streets of Whitehall, before leading the government of the day. I will walk heroically into the Cabinet room to see adults trying to use emergency slide rules (supplied by GCHQ) by tapping them vigorously with both thumbs and trying to swipe upwards.

However, before that moment comes, I have to face the hard reality that IT and I are stuck with each other, and we are going to have to find a way to co-exist.

Part of the problem is that I refused to engage in the early days of IT and set my face against it. Even then it must have frightened me, so by the time I realised that it wasn't going away I was already behind most of my compatriots. It was a bit like running an 800 metre race when everyone else was already 200 metres into it, and I'd deliberately put a couple of pebbles in my shoes to make it even more difficult – the pebbles being my bad attitude.

In the early days of technology, my colleagues and I were given the task, once a month, of inputting new product codes and deleting old ones. Most of the others seemed to find it easy enough, so I left my go until late in the evening when everyone else had gone home. Two hours later, I'd failed to do even the basic tasks and wanted to cry in frustration – and I couldn't go back to the start and regroup for another day. So, in desperation, I just pulled the plug out and ran away. This crashed part of the company's fragile infrastructure and caused an awful lot of work for what was then called the computer department – somehow, I didn't get sacked, but (result!) I was never asked to do it again. Thereafter, I stuck to pen and paper for everything I could, usually getting someone to print off my emails, scribbling a reply and giving them back to be sent out.

Eventually, the pressure to engage became too great and a friend took charge, sat me down and taught me the basics, following which I could send emails, had a rudimentary grasp of PowerPoint and, given about twenty-four hours and a calm environment, could generate a very simple Excel spreadsheet. I was up and running, though always shadowed by a deep and profound distrust.

What has followed has been over thirty years of keyboard fumbling and learning the joys of the internet – something which, remember, wasn't really a thing until the early 2000s. I've gone from the brick that was my Nokia phone through to being the last person on the planet to relinquish my BlackBerry and then to an uneasy, but practical, relationship with my iPhone. I don't really do social media as I'm convinced 'there be dragons' in the software, though I have to confess to a love of WhatsApp – especially for organising stuff and the odd, questionable joke. During this period, I've driven my family mad by constantly cocking things up, mainly because I get frustrated and start randomly pressing buttons – doubling the problem that needs fixing. I stomp around a lot, saying, 'Yes! But why does it do that?' Even recently, when trying to set up Apple Pay, there was a simple instruction to hold the phone up to the reader. I assumed I was the reader, so brought it up to my own face – I think my wife wet herself with laughter.

I'm a reasonably intelligent adult, so I've been steadfastly trying to understand the causes of these problems. Most are psychological flaws in me, though there is a small chamber in my heart that always will blame geeky programmers 5,000 miles away.

I hate the fact that something just stops working for absolutely no reason – if it was a car that stopped on the outside lane of the motorway and needed restarting, you wouldn't be happy. I have worked out that you need to actually read instructions on the screen, rather than skim them as men are renowned to do – but I have also learned what type of message you can just 'accept'.

Friends have convinced me to stop trying to work out why a computer does strange things. If you bought a toaster in the eighties or nineties, it tended to work in predictable ways, or if it didn't, you had a pretty good idea why – apparently, it's a fruitless waste of emotional energy to apply the same expectations to software. I've learned that you need to be accurate, which takes time, whereas I've always worked on the principle that 'near enough is good enough'. In the past the postman or shopkeeper would correct minor mistakes but software doesn't make those kinds of concessions. Finally, I've worked out that it's a control issue for me – I really struggle with a system that will passively refuse to work and I have no recourse. Often you find yourself caught on a page with no 'back' or enter' button, yet you've made a mistake that you have no idea how to fix. In short, an algorithm has dominion over you.

It also comes down to fear: fear of failure and fear of looking foolish; fear of accidentally sending all my money to a café in Kazakhstan; and fear of being scammed because I've opened the wrong email. The worst fear is the fear of fear itself, which manifests as anxiety about having to do anything on the computer or phone, with all the myriad ways such things could go wrong. Asking my wife to supervise key transactions is not really a long-term strategy.

I give myself a good talking to on a regular basis and I am making some headway. I'm understanding the problems and I've learned to take my time, be accurate and accept graciously when things go wrong. I'm pathetically pleased with myself when something works, although I still have the instinct to print off the details, just as proof or in case the *Day of the Triffids* unfolds.

Over time, I've mastered Amazon Prime and Booking.com and clearly a single WhatsApp message is so much more efficient than making ten calls when organising a group event. I can really see the benefits and I'm taking a much more grown-up approach to technology, although I don't think I'll ever get used to talking to a bot and AI scares the crap out of me. I grew up asking real people things and I desperately miss that, especially if there is a complaint or complicated problem. Maybe it's because I want human sympathy for my plight, or just to be heard by a person, but I can't help reflecting that individuals are now expected to be responsible for their own solutions even though they didn't cause the problem in the first place. I firmly believe that you get a much richer answer talking to people, though I do accept that some simple transactions are best handled without small talk.

If I have a worry, and as 'Analogue Man' I know that it may be self-serving, it would be the loss of human communication skills. There is value in passing the time of day, or asking the open question, that plays to our core psychological make-up. We need to be grounded by others seeing and experiencing the same things, or we lose perspective, given the complexity of modern life. We should be able to use the written word to convey emotions rather than rely on an emoji, which is just lazy. A phone call, or better still, a face-to-face over a coffee, reinforces what it is to be human. Technologically efficient communications come with their own loneliness or disconnection, especially with more of us working from home. For my generation, I suspect it is a significant risk, though I imagine it's a basic human issue across all age groups.

I'll end with a dystopian picture of my own house. Our heating system is fiendishly complicated and our entertainment setup requires the IT skills to hack Jodrell Bank. Our utilities and most of our assets have been set up by my wife, though paying the paper bill is a task I proudly hang on to. There are electronic systems everywhere, from ovens that need at least seven buttons pressed before you can reheat a cup of coffee, through to windows that open on a whim. If my wife ever leaves me, I'm screwed. After about six months, I'll be found by well-meaning friends, dressed in all my clothes for warmth, huddled around a candle, empty baked bean cans everywhere, newspapers all over the floor and a wind-up radio for company. So, it's that or I fully engage with the world of technology before it's too late.

Men and Women: Mars and Venus, or Just around the Corner?

For most people, really understanding the opposite sex is like trying to knit fog. Many of us will have been in a bar with a group of our own sex, shaking our heads and rolling our eyes at one of Mother Nature's most intriguing puzzles – the differences and similarities between men and women. My thinking is prompted by my own relationship, which both enhances and undermines any popular view of the sexes. My wife would rather chew off her arm than talk about her feelings, while I will blab about mine like a hormonal Girl Guide. She is eminently practical, whereas I'm utterly useless, and have dangerous tools gently taken off me and put out of reach. On the other hand, she is clearly a woman, as demonstrated by her empathy, thoughtfulness and ridiculous love of scatter cushions – something I believe no man will ever comprehend. Meanwhile, I typically exhibit many masculine tendencies: a love of contact sports, risk-taking and general laddish behaviour. I also confirm my masculinity with a complete inability to find my things around the house. My wife puts this down to the male history of scanning the horizon for wildebeests, rather than looking for berries right in front of the cave. I propose a 'scatter cushion' and 'sock-finding' index to help us make sense of the historical, evolutionary and social contexts that separate men from women.

In the meantime, until these indices have been established and peer reviewed, the 'big five' personality traits have already been helpfully identified by psychologists. They demonstrate a spectrum of personality types within broad categories which provide us with a good place to start understanding human nature. They form the top of a pyramid underpinned by more nuanced explanation. Qualities in each category also have their opposites; for example, empathy and manipulation are the Yin and Yang under the broad 'agreeableness' category.

The first category is 'openness', covering imagination, thought, curiosity and desire for new ideas and experiences. For this trait, there is little difference at the top level between men and women, though at the micro level, women tend to self-score higher on aesthetics and feelings, while men are stronger on ideas and perceived intellect. The intellect score, which again is self-rated, is often because men think they are cleverer than they are, though in extensive tests there are no significant intellectual differences between the sexes; this can possibly be attributed to male hubris and female humility.

The second identified trait is 'conscientiousness', which gives a more thoughtful, detailed, organised and goal-orientated individual. Again, the sexes are pretty consistent at the broad category level, though there is some evidence that, below this, women score higher on orderliness, and men on industriousness, perhaps as a hangover from male-dominated work environments.

The third personality trait is 'extroversion', which manifests as excitable, talkative, emotional, sociable and expressive character traits. Typically, category scores are more in favour of women, driven by the warmth and gregariousness metrics, while men major on assertiveness and excitement-seeking. These are all sub-sets of the extroversion category, demonstrating the complex nature of any top-line analysis and the need to drill down for greater insight.

'Agreeableness' is the fourth characteristic, exploring trust, altruism, empathy and affection for others. It is an area where women score consistently higher than men, highlighting their bias toward social engagement and compassion.

The final trait is 'neuroticism': an unfortunate word, given its pejorative contemporary use; academics can be clumsy. However, as expected, it covers the negative traits of moodiness, stress and emotional stability. It is biased towards women, though men score higher on anger and hostility.

We can all be broadly understood in these terms, with the huge caveat that it's complex, dynamic and open to our own biases. Complex because we are complex creatures, dynamic because we adapt, using different traits in different circumstances, and biased because we can't always separate out our own prejudices. It should be stressed that there is no right or wrong in character types; they just represent what we are. Categories are not value statements, because there is a time and a place for all types and skills. You wouldn't want to be flown by an airline pilot who measures high on openness and creativity, with scant regard for the details of how to land – although, in extremis, if you ever have to land a plane on the Hudson River, different ways of thinking might help. Conversely, you probably wouldn't use a conscientious accountant to design an opening ceremony for the Olympic Games, though you might need an army of them to actually deliver it.

As far as I'm concerned, these personality types do provide significant insight, and have really helped me understand my fellow humans. The figures are based on meta-analysis of over

23,000 people in twenty-six countries. The results were consistent across many nationalities, although they were more pronounced in western countries.

However, the above opens me up to the charge of 'No shit, Sherlock!' Much of this will reflect the general understanding and experiences of men and women in everyday life. We see some obvious distinctions between the sexes, but it's also clear that we have significantly more in common. In reality, most of the differences, statistically, are small to moderate, and we also know that we have the ability to adopt other personality traits, if required. Personalities are a complex combination of all the traits, just with individual biases. But the differences are important and, I will argue, can have a material effect on our mental and physical well-being.

Personality differences can clearly inform the debate about the distinctions between men and women, but biology – our physiological make-up – is obviously another important variable. Terminology is critical: sex is generally defined as a biological categorisation, driven primarily by the opportunity to reproduce, while gender is seen as a choice the individual makes to express their sexuality and identity in a social context. The debate on sex and gender differences is emotionally charged and contested, though both definitions are important when understanding relationships. Biologically, it's obvious that men and women are not the same, though the argument rages as to how much behaviour is influenced by nature or nurture. I'd contend that that is a pointless distinction – it is clearly both, so we are left to assess the balance between the two. Reproductive specialisation, or the rather clever ability to have babies, is an irrefutable difference in biology, and clearly it will have an effect on behaviour. Men's bodies typically have seventy-five percent more muscle mass and are demonstrably taller, stronger and heavier, with faster reaction times and more accurate throwing abilities. Added to this is the male's greater tolerance of risk, reinforcing men's evolution into the hunting and providing role. Women have adapted to be successful in the mating, child-bearing and socialisation game, looking for the best possible genes and protection during an unusually long pregnancy and a highly vulnerable rearing period thereafter. It's debatable who has the best deal – a 'quickie' at the back of the cave and then out to face woolly mammoths and sabre tooth tigers or years of nappies and taking the kids to hunting-and-gathering clubs at weekends.

Our biology is driven by our chromosomes, which, in the vast majority of cases, differentiate the sexes. In the womb, the male develops the XY chromosome, while in women it is the XX pattern that predominates. Additionally, you can add the influence of our hormones; for men, it's testosterone, with a smaller amount of oestrogen, while for women it tends to be the other way around. Our lived experience is within our bodies, and our minds, so, with such significant differences in our chromosomes, biological make-up and hormones, our behaviours are bound to be different. To a degree, the human species, like others, adapts, but it is not starting with a blank canvas. Please note that to ensure the long-term survival of the male sex, it's best not to mention hormones in an argument with your partner.

Socialisation, and the degree to which socialisation affects our gender-related behaviour is a debate that will continue to rage. Some will argue that the environment, and how we are brought up, will have a disproportionate impact, overriding many of the biological and pathological biases. A key factor in these beliefs is the longevity and explicit or implicit power of the patriarchy. This is something that is hard to argue against, when it's clear that men have dominated and abused their positions of power for thousands of years. Patriarchal dominance is something that is clearly wrong, but, putting this dominance all down to socialisation is open to challenge and is riddled with unintended consequences. It implies that if we work on society's attitudes and actions alone, ignoring the biological and personality biases, we can solve deeply embedded inequality issues. If, as I do, you accept that there are fundamental differences between men and women, then we have to understand that these will impact society differently. Men can potentially exhibit greater aggression or carelessness, so accommodation or control of their behaviour needs to reflect that, for example in education, where the learning patterns of boys and girls can be seen to vary widely.

However, and in support of the socialisation argument, there has been interesting work on the big five personality traits, and how they are assessed. If people are asked to self-report on character types, they will often inadvertently accentuate gender stereotypes. When more sophisticated, indirect and observational techniques are used, the differences between the sexes are significantly diminished. This can be seen in multiple studies where, if people self-report, there is about a twenty-five percent difference in personality traits between men and women, which falls to only eight percent if more subtle tests are used that don't rely on self-assessment. Demonstrably, our biases and social influences run very deep which, in turn, makes people more susceptible to ideologies and deep self-interest.

Instinctively, we can all understand that if we are brought up, especially in our early years, with gender stereotypes, we are much more likely to demonstrate gender-specific behaviours. If boys have guns and cars and girls have dolls and cuddly toys, they will want more of the same, conforming to the stereotypes of expected male and female roles and strengths. Bizarrely, my mother refused to get me an Action Man because she thought it constituted 'playing with dollies'. Maybe she was just trying to correct my nascent female traits or maybe she simply failed to understand the concept of Action Man. Whatever, I think I have got over it now. I also have a vivid memory of trying to play dolls' house with my young daughter who, after realising that I don't do imagination, summarily dismissed me before going in search of her mother. And so, we are stuck in a repeating cycle of behavioural norms – girls will feel the pressure to behave like girls, boys will want to behave like boys, and parents and/or schools will perpetuate the cycle. There are deep psychological reasons why we play in different ways but there are also deep societal pressures that accentuate these differences. Addressing one and not the other will only give half the answer.

As we get further from the womb, the legitimacy of the argument for the power of socialisation strengthens. Boys and girls will have many more influences coming at them, and the pressure to conform increases. School friends, families, teachers, the media, books and manly-doll manufacturers, potentially, push children into behaviours and attitudes that don't sit naturally with them. With this, the system prevails and, the argument goes, the insidious or overt patriarchal power continues; with thousands of years of experience, why would this not be the case?

However, there is not yet compelling evidence that children left more to their own devices will eschew some of the stereotypes we visit on them. Boys, though more socialised, will still choose toys that play to their interest in movement and girls will gravitate to toys with faces – independent choices that get stronger as they get older. The reasons are based on biology or socialisation or a combination of the two – so, rather like separating the ingredients of a cooked omelette, good luck with identifying the component parts. Our friends, parents, media and society generally will heavily influence behaviour, which, at the same time, is fighting or complementing our core humanity.

And there begins a lifetime struggle between our true natures and what our environment expects from us.

We are all subject to our lived experience on the male/female continuum and I consider myself to be very lucky in this department. I grew up in a family that implicitly recognised the differences and valued all, equally. As far back as the 1960s, my mother wouldn't have dreamed of being given housekeeping and, unusually for the time, my parents operated a joint bank account. My father was still the practical one, a trait bred out in my case, and my mother did most of the child care, but it was, and is, a relationship of equals. Maybe because of this background, or just something I worked out along the way, I have always enjoyed working with women. In my experience, women tend to operate with their brains, not their egos, which makes decision-making so much easier. I've seen many more men whose bottom lip will be quivering if they don't get the right company car than I've seen destructive emotions from women in business. Obviously, there are exceptions but it emphasises how wrong stereotypes can be, and how we should identify the best in each other first. Many of us live in relationships and observe relationships in others, so we all see how they can work or, sadly, not work.

The real question is, does any of this matter and should we

carry on muddling through, with men and women treated simply as people. Do gender roles need to be separated and responded to differently? I would contend that there is a very real need to work with the differences, while recognising our complementary abilities, and enjoying the overwhelming similarities. Clearly, for people with non-binary gender identities, this is particularly important, and loaded with huge health and happiness issues if not approached properly; while numbers may be small, they do represent the canary in the coal mine of sexual and gender tolerance. More traditional identities of women and men will still benefit from tailored interventions and the recognition from society of key differences. I will pick out some of the specifics for men, as it's an area of special interest, but the principles are important for both genders.

Boys typically will mature and develop later than girls. They can have higher energy, and, with reduced capacity for concentrated learning, they fidget. Boys' reading skills develop later, so they can be disadvantaged because the ability to read is critical to studying other subjects, such as STEM subjects (Science, Technology, Engineering and Maths). One in twelve males is colour-blind, compared to one in two hundred females, so there are very specific challenges that, if not addressed, can lead to lack of confidence and withdrawal – imagine explaining a concept with bar charts or Venn diagrams when someone can't differentiate the colours.

Men have materially higher tendencies towards crime or substance abuse, part of which is societal, but part of which is driven by behavioural traits, like greater risk-taking. Men perpetuate most violence, but are also the primary victims of most violence. Men die earlier and are more subject to non-sexually specific cancers, while the majority of people who find themselves homeless are men. It's well documented that the ratio of suicides of men to women is three to one, and that suicide is a significant problem in young men, who struggle to find their way in a world that, amongst other things, has high expectations of specific kinds of 'masculine' behaviour, expectations that encourage self-reliance and discourage emotional weakness. Men are more likely to bottle up feelings, play to the expectation of controlling their emotions, and adhere to society's stereotype of competence and strength. On top of these, there are specific male-orientated medical issues like prostate cancers or reduced testosterone, which may present in behavioural ways. Hopefully, a lot of the above can be reduced, solved or ameliorated by specific interventions tailored towards men and boys – in education, mental health, medicine or dealing with societal pressures. The role of masculinity in all this is a subject for another essay, but it will clearly demonstrate that society needs to attend to the differences. Of course, the same is the case for women, who will equally need tailored interventions in specific circumstances.

In conclusion, I believe there are huge similarities between the male and female of our species. We both walk on two legs, need to eat and drink, stay warm, are social creatures; we are geared to reproduce effectively and probably all need love, self-esteem and purpose. In our personalities, the differences are relatively small, and both sexes have learned to adopt different traits for different circumstances. We are not from different planets but from just around the corner.

So, it's in that context that I highlight the differences, whether driven by personality, evolution, biology or social conditioning. These differences, while being smaller in number, are important, and dedicated interventions like education, health and social conditioning will benefit many men and, arguably, a society of all the genders. Men and women have found ways of working together for the good of both throughout history, so a little mutual appreciation may help. It does, however, require a massive act of partial forgiveness by women for the patriarchy, its oppression and suppression over time – a forgiveness that should be heavily qualified and very warily bestowed. The 'battle of the sexes', as parodied, is destructive, and, while I hope we can still tease each other, it should not be taken seriously – partly because, as Henry Kissinger put it, 'Nobody will ever win the battle of the sexes. There's too much fraternizing with the enemy.'

The Pecking Order

Let me introduce our chickens – they are the luckiest in the country, living as they do in a fox-resistant fortress, with freedom to roam (and crap) during the day. They all have names, so there is no chance of them ending up on a dinner plate. Conservatively, I'd estimate that it has cost us about five pounds an egg over many years. Bluebell is the most inappropriately named, because she is the big bruiser and the enforcer of the group – occasionally she's called Mike Tyson, which is a much better fit for her personality. I suspect the 'thought leader' is Dotty, who is strident, bossy and self-important – the Ann Widdecombe of the poultry world. Next is Punkie, who looks like Vyvyan from *The Young Ones* and sports a ginger Mohican. In truth, she is a bit timid and hides behind Bluebell, but she does look angry most of the time – maybe she is passive-aggressive? My personal favourite is Plucky-Lucky, because I saved her from certain death, finding her in the field twenty-four hours after a bid for freedom. Hence the Lucky bit. The Plucky comes from her unpredictable flights of aggression – she will suddenly shoot out of the run, wings spinning and scatter the otherwise peaceful group. She is a bit like the skinny kid in school whom no-one bullies because they might just stab you in the eye with a pair of compasses. Finally, we have Nugget who, as well as being named after a chicken dish, is the weakest of the flock and the most susceptible to bullying. However, when she runs, it's a crazy blur of legs and wings, as if she has a lit Catherine Wheel stuck on each side – I often creep out and throw food to the other side of the garden, just to see her run.

Chickens are flock birds, so form a little society, in this case without the encumbrance of a male. There is bullying and positioning in the pecking order, so much so that we've had to get them all together, and talk it through. A previous flock had a couple of persistent bullies who, in the end, had to be deported to North Devon (by car; they weren't expected to make their own way). The chickens' days have rituals and special places to scratch and feed, though they live in eternal hope that, every time we open the back door, there might be a treat to be had. If there *are* treats – they especially like spaghetti – they behave very badly. One will swoop on a beakful of pasta and make a run for it, with all the others giving chase. Even though there is more than enough to go around, they must have the other girl's plunder.

But then they will also look out for each other, cuddle up in the cold, or warn one and all in case of danger – often sending Bluebell out in front, with a look on her face of 'come on, if you think you're hard enough'. They have their own microcosm of chicken society and it's constantly changing as new chickens come and go – the living embodiment of the 'pecking order'. I love them for their personalities, their permanent presence and their silly walks, though I live in fear of forgetting to lock them up at night and them falling prey to public enemy number one – the fox. They are a responsibility and a joy, and I probably worry about them more than I worry about my kids.

Nicknames and Banter

I have had many nicknames over the years, notably based on my middle name of Stanley, which is enough of a curse in its own right. I had my front teeth knocked out about the time a toothless Stan Bowles was playing for Queens Park Rangers – and the name 'Stan' stuck. Then we had the Falklands war, bringing Port Stanley to public prominence, which, when combined with my dubious ability to balance a pint on my gut, led to Portly Stanley. Then 'Portly' which has stuck, despite having a new set of teeth, losing my gut and being an age when we should all know better.

I've always loved nicknames, but have often wondered why people use them, given that most recipients have a perfectly serviceable name from birth. I was inspired by an analysis of nicknames from an obscure university in Nebraska, USA – maybe there isn't so much to do in Nebraska? – and I've combined this with reading research on male banter and the results of an open brief to friends who have fed me good nicknames they have come across. The only thing I've excluded is pet names between consenting adults. If you decide to call your partner something, or worse still, name a part of their anatomy, you are honour-bound to keep it to yourself – other people at the party will thank you for it.

I think the first category of nicknames should be around things that you do or have done. One of my favourites is a Second World War military family. Out of four brothers, two were awarded the Victoria Cross (one posthumously), one was awarded the Military Cross and the undecorated fourth brother was affectionately nicknamed 'The Coward'. A good friend got himself a reputation for rummaging through his wash bag and offering up the wrong pills or powders for a range of minor illnesses – so was inevitably called 'Shipman'. Also, in the same group of friends, there is an appallingly bad motorbike rider, known to everyone as 'Dead Graham', as, and we keep telling him, it's only a matter of time.

My second category is around behavioural traits or qualities. A guy we cycle with never stops to help anyone with a breakdown or a puncture. We call him 'Concordia', referencing the captain who left his sinking ship before his passengers. Then there's the guy who had a bad limp, whom we called 'Sniper's nightmare'. I had a colleague called 'Storm Lantern' because he never went out. In college, I knew a girl who had the most appalling sense of direction, and was forever late because she was always getting lost; 'Columbus' just seemed to fit and it stuck. Probably the most innocuous-sounding but ultimately damning one was a teenager called 'Lacklustre'. I hope it was ironic.

As a subset of behavioural names, there are those intended to burnish a reputation or reinforce a character type. I suspect 'Vlad the Impaler' would not have been so famous as 'Vladimir the Not Very Nice'. Margaret Thatcher must have had more impact as 'the Iron Lady' than she would have done had she been known as 'The Mule' instead. And while I think Donald Trump is an appalling human being, he does get credit for his outstandingly negative use of nicknames, which stick and undermine his opponents, including 'Crooked Hillary', 'Lyin' Ted Cruz' and 'Sleepy Joe Biden' which are a small part of a whole Wikipedia page on the subject. Still, as one of his supporters said on TV, 'He's a genius – that's what the 'J' in Donald J Trump stands for.'

Physical characteristics are one of the most obvious categories and hunting grounds for nicknames. John, a rough-and-ready carpet fitter from Croydon, had half his ear bitten off in a fight. I've no idea what his real surname is, and I suspect most of his mates don't either, because everyone just calls him 'John Van Gogh'. There is a famous nickname from the Welsh Valleys for a guy with only one tooth in the front of his mouth: known to all as 'Dai Central Eating'. I just hope he was a plumber. 'Vaughan the Prawn' had a small willy, though he seemed unembarrassed answering to the name. I'm indebted to Jeremy Clarkson for a few examples of nicknames from his past, one of the best being a boy born with one hand smaller than the other – inevitably called 'Clock'. But my all-time favourite in this group is 'Biscuit'. The chap's name was Gary and he was bald.

Names and derivatives of names are easy pickings. Clarkson's first two are Baxter Campbell, who was called 'Two Soups', and Wayne Bruce, who was named 'Manbat'. Think about it. A college friend, Chris May, is forever called 'April May', while John Voyle is best known as 'Olive'. With a surname like Mutton you had to be known as Geoff, and anyone with the innocuous surname of Davison is crying out to be called 'Harley'. Another friend, with the double-barrelled surname initials of BJ, got to be called 'Blowie', but my favourite in this category is Dick Holder, who could only ever be 'Jock Strap'. What were his parents thinking?

There is some debate about the origin of nicknames, but the most credible is that it was to hide your identity from the devil or 'Old Nick' – hence nicknames. Throughout history, and across social classes, I hope and believe we use nicknames as a demonstration of liking. This is especially true for men who can use them to show affection without breaking masculine behavioural codes. Names confer membership of the tribe or social group, from the sports team to the street gang. In addition, they are a way of keeping your mates' feet on the ground – no one is allowed to get above themselves, or they will end up with a well-meaning poke in the eye, via a new name.

It must also be recognised that nicknames can be abusive and designed to belittle. They can enforce uncomfortable power relationships if they are bestowed with malice. Dishing out and enjoying nicknames has to be the prerogative of all in the group and not the select few – or they quickly become divisive and hurtful. I'm sure some people use them offensively, or to make themselves feel superior to others, but I like to believe that those people are in the minority.

My exhaustive study, aka asking my sisters and observing women in their natural habitat, shows it's much more of a male trait. Women don't tend to participate, either because it can be used in a bitchy way, or it's just too silly a habit to waste time on.

Banter is the mothership of nicknames, because it allows men to just take the piss out of each other, and from that, some new names are born – though this is not a prerequisite. A nickname is for life while banter is ongoing and continuous. It has been defined as 'to speak or to address in a witty and teasing manner', but, thereafter, it's hard to pin down as a phenomenon. It also, now, comes with its own baggage, for its role in abuse and jokes that go too far. Barbed banter, often racist or homophobic, which upsets or excludes people, should be called out for what it is: abuse. It also means that we have to be alert to misinterpretation by the recipient who, even though the comment was meant in good humour, is genuinely upset.

On the positive side, it can help inject a little fun into the boredom of a tedious situation, demonstrate a point, enable socialisation and recognise or enjoy differences. It's also a significant stress reliever, merging with gallows humour as a way of getting a group through a difficult situation. Again, it's mainly a male thing, and although some women are good at joining in banter, it doesn't seem to be their 'go-to' technique – which opens it up to the possible charge of exclusion, especially in the workplace. It's been said that men bond by insulting each other, but they really don't mean it, while women bond by complimenting each other, but they really don't mean it. I would not advocate any type of exclusion, but I would recognise the social benefits of bonding for men. I observe the phenomenon in Western or English-speaking countries and I see it in all age groups. We learn it growing up and hone the skills in social settings, always looking to get our retaliation in first. Banter is an art form for my son's twenty-something generation, even being shortened to 'bant' – presumably to avoid the time-consuming effort of the syllable 'er'?

Banter can be categorised in similar ways to nicknames, and with the same objective of making people laugh. It may be something in the recipient's name or physical characteristics, but it's most often highlighting something dumb that someone has said or done. Unlike nicknames, which take some thinking about and some time to bed in, banter is much more continuous. Think of it as planes coming in to Heathrow, with opportunities for jokes in each one. They are continually landing and from all directions. Some will touch down and take off again for the fun of circling a couple more times, and some can have short- or long-haul lifespans. However, no approach or landing is ever wasted, as they can always be used another day in another way. Maybe the same thing will happen again, so you can start to see the holy grail of banter – namely, a pattern. Sometimes two unrelated piss-takes can be stitched together, which is a great skill, needing considerable experience to execute well. Additionally, remember that it's a game for everyone, so while you're thinking of something funny, others may be ahead of you and your vulnerable soft underbelly is exposed – because the number one rule of banter is you live by the sword, you die by the sword.

So, while I await the call from the Nobel organisation for academic rigour in the study of nicknames and banter, I'll continue to promote their value and diversity. They are usually fun, often very witty and hopefully a sign of human warmth or affection – especially for men, with our sex's stunted emotional development. Long may they continue.

Political Correctness and Humour:
an Incomplete Reflection

What makes one person belly laugh and leaves another one cold? Or what might one find funny while someone else is left offended and bruised? These are age-old questions given extra life by our current social mores and the prevailing attitudes that enforce political correctness. What follows examines humour in context and is absolutely not a classic rant about 'political correctness gone mad' – that would be too easy. It will look at how we reconcile, or don't reconcile, the use of humour and the risk of offence.

Humour is defined as a type of action, speech or written word that amuses, covering social interactions that are ridiculous, jocular, surprisingly odd, or comic. We all know it when we see it and respond to it – it makes us laugh or smile. Simplistically, humour comes at us in four main ways: jokes which are predesigned; funny anecdotes that people pass around, from the caveman's fire to the WhatsApp group; spontaneous humour that is actively created during everyday conversation and actions, from banter to slapstick; and purely accidental stuff that just bubbles up, like a verbal misunderstandings or banana-skin slips, when no-one was looking for it. To find something funny, we need our intellect to understand it, and a sense of irreverence or disruption to appreciate the illogicality of the situation. We are then rewarded with the emotional high of spontaneous laughter.

What fascinates me most are the social benefits and dynamics of humour, because this is how we manage ourselves and communicate with our fellow man. There have been hundreds of studies and attempts to categorise humour, but I will try to synthesise them under the categories of incongruity, superiority, and relief – though as with most categorisations, it is impossible to cover everything, including the overlaps between them.

Some humour comes from crazy or incongruous events or situations, and how we interpret them, followed by how we explain and build a narrative around the nonsense. This kind of humour feeds off a complex world where mistakes and misconceptions are everyday events: 'A funny thing happened to me on the bus today'. Appreciation of the downright silly goes across both sexes and is part of the joy of being human, yet the motivations for finding something funny no doubt differ. Both sexes enjoy humour for its own sake, but for men it allows us to show the child in us, even though we are meant to be grown up. It demonstrates that we don't take ourselves too seriously, despite the trappings of masculine competence – it's a social signal that we want to be playful. Men do silly really well, especially if you get a group of like-minded blokes together. Women may roll their eyes at our buffoonery but I hope they are laughing with us rather than at us.

Some humour is disparaging, allowing the observer to feel superior. If someone makes a fool of themselves or suffers an ignominious failure, it can be funny, especially if you're not implicated. It's even more fun if you don't like the unfortunate individual, though it's still worth a chuckle if it's a friend. This also extends to group behaviour and can emphasis the in-group and out-group dynamics, as in 'There was this Irishman...'. This type of humour is dangerous because it can lead to exclusion and bullying, so it treads a fine line. It's especially pernicious because unpleasantness can be wrapped up in such a way as to give the perpetrator a way out: 'Only joking'. We use humour for establishing power relationships, cementing our positions and pushing others down the hierarchy. Now that we no longer use overt Silverback Gorilla behaviour, a well-chosen, funny put-down can be just as effective as a 'How red is my bottom?' display.

Most of us would recognise humour as a lubricant for group activities, male and female. It can be used to de-stress a situation or relieve boredom in other circumstances. Gallows humour, and a sense of the ridiculous, can turn a bad situation around, playing, as it does, to our deep-seated knowledge of our fallibility – we are all a bit ridiculous, and so is the world we inhabit. Similarly, waiting in a line at the bank or being inactive in a fire station cries out for the free entertainment that joking gives.

Additionally, humour is a powerful social conduit. It can convey the type of person you are, and what motivates you, while probing for more information about the other individual. It can be a dance to establish your acceptance into a group by complying with the established style of humour – or it can give you very clear messages about what the group, or key individuals, will and won't tolerate. And it does all this in a light-hearted way. A joke and comment can be withdrawn, or left to wither, without social consequences, but direct comments or opinions are much more permanent and dangerous. In short, humour can help us find our tribe, and function in many disparate tribes.

Humour serves many purposes, but also involves the simple pleasure of joking and having fun with our fellow man – it should not be over-thought. It is a very basic characteristic of our species and, while some primates may have a go at it, it does seem to be a fundamentally human thing. It adds joy, warmth and the cathartic pleasure of laughing out loud, in harmony with others.

It's been said that 'Humour is a source of power and healing and may be key to our survival' (Gregg, 2002). It's clearly been shown to be more than just laughing at someone slipping on a banana-skin. We are highly sophisticated, social creatures that use humour in many complex and varied ways. From the King's Fool to *Spitting Image*, humour has the ability to lampoon those who seek dominion over us and to heal our emotional wounds. It's part of our success as a species, as well as being one of the best things about our lives. Whether and how it should be controlled are the key questions to be addressed.

For good, or bad, one of the constraints on humour has been 'political correctness'. Originally it emerged in Marxist/Leninist vocabulary, with the explicit intention of ensuring adherence to the party line. Its current incarnation came into being in the mid-seventies, as a way of preventing the abuse of marginalised groups. The phrase 'political correctness' became a pejorative term in the early nineties, causing mature adults to grab their pearls and tut – a primarily right-wing reaction to perceived soft liberalism. At its simplest, it's a formal way of enforcing the standards that society prefers. More positively, it's a thoughtful use of language, designed not to offend, belittle or disadvantage individuals or groups. It has improved communication in society: we now pay attention to racist abuse; we are embarrassed by the use of sexist or patriarchal language; gay rights are protected in law; and jokes at the expense of disabled people are no longer acceptable. All good; in fact, great, and an example of constrained speech – so where does that leave other possible subjects for fun and laughter?

As an example, I will use a light-hearted piece I wrote about a boys' cycling trip to Istanbul. Firstly, I complained about my travelling mate's 'poofy' tyres which kept getting punctures; it was meant to be funny because it painted a picture of flappy, rather ineffectual kit, as opposed to the rugged, macho tyres that I had. I was taking the piss out of my friend, and bigging up my own choices, in a flippant way, but a few people I respect have blanched at the reference. I like to think I would say the same to a gay friend, although I guess I would now be sensitive to any adverse reaction. In no way would I be trying to undermine or offend, but I have an unanswered question in my mind about how many would be offended – just the thin-skinned or a significant proportion? I feel really conflicted on the subject because I hate to upset anyone, but also a little sad that what was meant without malice results in less room for fun. Are well-meaning motivations enough to compensate for possible offence? I hope so.

Secondly, I euphemistically used 'beaver' references in my writing as it had become one of the running jokes on the trip, probably still influenced by the famous scene in *Airplane* when a stuffed beaver was the centre of a wonderfully silly *double entendre*. Of course, the term refers to women in coarse language, but many find its naughtiness funny, including, and in particular, my travelling companion – though it's especially ironic in his case because he's singularly unsuccessful with women. I wonder if women have a similarly derogatory and silly range of sexualised words to refer to men. I can't think of any off the top of my head, but I strongly suspect the delicate male ego would be shocked if it knew. The problem with my sex is we are too obvious and guileless in our desires, while women are much cleverer about it.

There is, of course, the 'snowflake' defence: the argument that people shouldn't be so thin-skinned or take themselves any more seriously than the writer or speaker intended. This only holds a certain amount of water, especially if people feel they are genuinely being belittled.

The follow-up to this is 'where does it end'? Do LGBTQ sensitivities get extended until we run out of letters of the alphabet and everyone is categorised, and therefore 'protected'? Are we no longer allowed to comment on someone's appearance or stupid actions? Is piss-taking to be banned completely, in which case most men would lose fifty percent of their conversation? The logical conclusion is that we will only be telling 'why did the chicken cross the road' jokes in the hope that chickens aren't offended and have got more important things to worry about.

Finally, we have the '18-rated' argument: if you don't want to see sex and violence, don't go and see an 18-rated film. It's your choice. A book about three middle-aged blokes on a cycling trip is unlikely to be decorous or sophisticated. I find this argument has much to commend it, though it's not water-tight.

Things tend to need a pendulum swing to shake society up and language is part of that. Perhaps political correctness goes further than necessary, by changing our vocabulary to establish a point. I doubt if, in a few years' time, we will be still 'taking the knee' regularly for Black Lives Matter but our awareness of the issue is much higher than if we had simply followed society's normally slow trajectory: a trajectory that could, rightly, no longer tolerate *The Black and White Minstrel Show* or Alf Garnett, but gives open space to comedians such as Frankie Boyle et al. Language has made a positive difference.

At the end of this essay, I'm still heavily conflicted, though I propose to leave 'poofy' tyres and 'beavers' in my book – along with many other questionable references. A big part of my motivation was to make people laugh and, while the iterations may be puerile, I think they're funny. I can search my conscience and be sure that there was no malice or offence even considered – in reality, I don't think any of us thought about it that deeply. Humour is a big part of what it is to be a human being, underpinning our social frameworks for both men and women. Certainly, the sexes sometimes execute humour in different ways, and for different reasons, but it's part of us and controlling it may be a Sisyphean task. Others may disagree, and see a sensitivity to language as a prerequisite for a caring, inclusive community. I have a number of friends who think this way, and, for sure, they have a point.

I Bear-Sprayed the Dog

When exploring the Yukon, it's worth remembering that you are no longer top of the food chain. There are many opportunities to die prematurely, especially at the hands (or teeth) of bears, who have a deserved reputation for being grumpy, so I was pretty careful when out and about – except for this one time.

I was out for a walk in remote and wild mountain terrain, with only the lead husky for company. He was a fabulous specimen whose genes and attitude to life had singled him out as first amongst equals, taking the front berth in a top winter-husky team under the direction of our guide, Almon. Good as the dog was, I didn't want to rely on him taking one for the team (i.e. me) if we were confronted by some of the Yukon's more exotic inhabitants, so it had seemed best to take the bear spray, even though I had no idea how to use it. But having the tin in my hand was like having an itch – and I found myself wondering 'how does it work and shouldn't I have a practice in case there is a real bear incident?'

It was one of those times when my brain didn't have time to get in front of my actions. I unhooked the safety clip and aimed at the far bushes. It essentially exploded in my hand and fired a huge jet of brown, atomised liquid about 15 or 20 metres. It smelled and looked a bit like balsamic vinegar and followed a very pleasing arc before splattering into dense vegetation. A bear's nose is reported to be 800 times more sensitive than a human's, so, if you aim it right, this spray is your best chance of buying time to escape. However, it's not great for dogs, and, in my preoccupation with the bear spray, I'd failed to notice that Almon's favourite – and very valuable – husky had disappeared behind those very bushes, minding its own business.

It hurtled out in shock, running towards me and rubbing its face in mid-flight, looking nothing like the considered and calm dog I'd started the walk with. It then flung itself on the ground in front of me, doing impromptu headstands as it tried to rub the spray off its nose. It beat its paws against its face while I stood in paralysed panic, with the growing realisation that I might have seriously damaged a champion lead husky. How the hell was I going to explain that to Almon? At about the same time, my brain caught up with my actions, and there was a parallel thought emerging that I might well have used all the bear spray – and I was pretty sure it was our only can.

So, in one dumb movement, I'd damaged a $1,000 dog and put the rest of us in danger for the remainder of the trip. I was transported back to that horrible feeling you have as a kid when you've done something really stupid and have no idea what to do next. It's the feeling of a seven-year-old queuing for an ice cream and wetting himself all over the floor – I know because I was that seven-year-old, and I can still feel the shame and shock, and see the look of horror on the café owner's face as I turned on my heels and fled. While the dog contorted in front of me, my desperate instinct was to run back to camp, confess everything and throw myself on the mercy of the group. I was fifty-seven, for God's sake, and I was seven all over again in the space of ninety seconds.

My fellow travellers from the camp came up to join me a few minutes after my crime, only to find me wild-eyed and gibbering about having to get back to Almon. My brain was screeching round corners and I was failing to put recognisable sentences together – I just had to get away. Fortunately, the dog seemed to have recovered, so I decided that that bit of the story was going to be our little secret. However, I had to find out if I'd really screwed up by using up our only bear spray. By the time I got back to the camp, I'd lost all self-control and just blabbed to Almon – even though my mate, Duncan, was sitting in easy earshot. Almon seemed pretty untroubled and we agreed that there was probably enough in the can for an emergency, so I was mightily relieved. I thought that was the end of it. Duncan, however, had stored the information away for use at a time of his choosing. He had an instinct that I'd dropped out of the category of adult behaviour and that I deserved to get my comeuppance for all to see.

With the unerring skill of a natural-born piss-taker, Duncan bided his time and launched the attack after the third pint, in a bar in the town of White Horse. I'd had time to prepare my defence, but, in the end, I was defenceless. I'd gone back to being a child in both the execution of the crime and the reaction to it – and Duncan wasn't even aware of the dog issue – but by this point I'd decided to spill all and throw myself on the mercy of the team. I think it was the only topic of conversation for the rest of that evening and for most of the seventeen-hour flight home. But it isn't the piss-taking or the craziness of the whole thing that fascinates me. It is, firstly, the capacity of a grown man to do incredibly dumb things, and, secondly, the speed by which you can go from being a mature and sophisticated adult to a massively embarrassed child – praying to the gods to turn back time and make it not have happened. Maybe it's comforting to know that our guilt reactions are so close to the surface, but it's also kind of worrying how quickly I unravelled in the face of a potential crisis. Maybe this wasn't so much of a crisis and I am, or will be, better when it counts, but it is a useful reminder that our thin layers of adult sophistication are just that: thin.

Cancer: Diagnosis and the Worst Bit

While at work, I got a call from my doctor with a stark message: 'David – it's bad news, I'm afraid. What we've found is a secondary cancer and we don't know where the primary is.' It felt as though my stomach, intestines and main organs were suddenly sucked out of my body, leaving me completely hollowed out, dazed and shockingly aware of what he had just said. My legs felt like they couldn't hold my weight and I crumpled from within – as when demolition experts implode an old power station. It was a deep and visceral sickness, rising with the bile in my throat: a feeling of vulnerability that was so profound it still shocks me to this day.

I managed to finish the call in what I thought was a grown-up way, saying all the sort of things that one is supposed to say in this situation. 'I'm going to fight it.' 'What do I do now to have the best chance?' 'Thank you for telling me – it can't have been easy for you saying that.' Then I prowled around my office for about ten minutes without thinking and without feeling. Bad stuff was just outside me and I was simply functioning.

I knew I had to call Caroline, but she had no idea I even had a problem, let alone that I'd had a biopsy. I can't remember any of the words but I do remember getting three or four sentences in, then breaking up. My voice went and I was crying like a child, trying to get the words out in between great heaving sobs. All she kept saying was, 'Come home, please come home,' while I was trying to get things out in the open before they ate me up – what were the worst case possibilities? And what this was going to mean for the children?

Before I left, I bizarrely had a sensible conversation with our French Sales Director about a customer discount proposal and followed this with a polite but cursory chat with the Marketing Director on my way down the stairs.

On the drive to the M25, the anger kicked in for the first and last time in the whole process. I didn't think it felt unfair and I wasn't feeling sorry for myself, but it was just going to hurt so many people, especially my kids. I was crying and begging to whoever was on high – 'Five more years, please, just give me five more years.'

That was over five years ago, so I'm ahead of the game.

The journey home was akin to operating in two parallel worlds. There was the bad stuff which was there but just floating around me in the car, and there was the functional me, driving purely to get home. It was a remarkably safe and surreal place to be in for about an hour. Then the slap of reality as I got home and found myself standing in our kitchen opposite Caroline, crying uncontrollably and saying, 'But I've got kids' over and over again.

Somehow, we managed to get through the afternoon but I needed to see my doctor that evening before a scan the next day. Strangely, I needed to hear it again but I also needed to be prepared for what the possibilities could be. I was full of questions. What if it's in the lungs? Can they operate? Where do squamous cells typically turn to next in the body? Could it be because I smoked cigars when I was younger? Of course, he didn't have many answers but he gave me his full attention and that was enough. Then I went home and googled it to truly scare the shit out of myself. I needed to know just how bad this could be, even though I only understood about twenty percent of what I was reading. At the same time, Caroline was researching it properly, but had the sense and kindness not to share any half facts with my fracturing brain.

The next morning was the scan. We went together, consciously trying to distract ourselves with the simple task of walking. I was trying to hold on to the numb feeling for safety, knowing that this was one of the most important hours of my life. Knowing it, but not wanting to acknowledge it. I don't have any memory of the scan; I just remember sitting opposite my lovely Iraqi consultant watching every nuance of his face as he scanned the screen. I was trying desperately to read in his eyes what he was seeing. The words he said were something like, 'Well, it's not in the lungs and I think the main organs are clear. But there is something in the tonsillar fissure.' Then something about 'I'm a lot happier about this,' and the tension broke. I stopped squeezing my fist which was leaving deep nail imprints the base of my palm, and allowed myself to breathe. With my other hand I was holding Caroline's, which was something we rarely did. However, it looked like better news and we feasted hungrily on whatever he said next. I wasn't out of the woods and may never be safe, but I had a chance. And that chance was all I had hoped for when I had walked in that morning.

Twenty hours had passed and I'd been turned inside out. I'd experienced profound emotion when facing real mortality, not just the abstract concept. This was real, terrifying and bewildering. I wasn't brave, I wasn't grown-up, and I was a frightened animal experiencing feelings of the most excruciating vulnerability. Nothing could ever have prepared me for that.

That evening we went to a shabby chic gin bar and afterwards to the theatre with friends – pleasantly surprised to be functioning. In fact, functioning well enough to go to a Gilbert O'Sullivan concert the next night and get a laugh out of Caroline by whispering that there were 'worse things in life than cancer'.

Within four days I'd had all the first set of scans and met two of the top consultants. I was told that surviving my cancer had an eighty or ninety percent chance of success; I'd caught it relatively early, and I was young enough and fit enough to face the treatment. Everyone was positive and we allowed ourselves guarded optimism... I could be one of the lucky ones.

The treatment was going to be fairly brutal, though I didn't hear or understand quite how brutal it was going to be. Maybe this was deliberate from the consultants on a 'best-not-to-know' basis or maybe it was the result of a scrabbled mind – I suspect a bit of both. There were more tests, a lot of needles stuck in me and a full biopsy. There were also many dark nights lost in the labyrinth of my own brain, and endless 'what if' conversations between me and Caroline. I was also stupidly trying to plan work commitments and family stuff, while trying to act as normally as possible for everyone to see.

Then came the worst bit.

We had to tell the kids and we had no idea how we were going to do that. I'd had to tell a couple of key people in work beforehand, so at least I'd tried out a kind of script. We had left it as late as we could, so we knew most of the facts, but there were no more excuses to put it off.

We settled on a Monday evening and I could think of little else or keep much food down for the whole day. I drove home, practising what I was going to say, feeling sick to my stomach. Then it just didn't happen. They had homework to do and everyone was in and out in a normal school-night kind of way. The pressure had been unbearable and I now had to go to bed with an ugly cloud hanging over me.

Finally, it had to be Wednesday evening, with a repeat of Monday's inevitable turmoil – no better and no worse, just awful. I called them both into the kitchen and started the script while watching, horrified, as their faces showed the enormity and fear that was coming hard at them. I think it was Daniel who interrupted me and said, 'Do you mean you have cancer?' It's a word I'd stupidly avoided using but the only answer was 'Yes'. Everything after that was lost in a cocktail of raw emotion that, even long after the event, takes a lot of piecing together. Daniel punched a cupboard and Lowri, I think, retreated to the other side of the room. All of us were crying and I was babbling through the speech, repeating over and over that it was going to be okay. You spend your life trying not to hurt your kids, then you knowingly and deliberately have to cause them deep pain and fear. It broke my heart and it's a picture I'll never forget. The last thing I remember in the kitchen was Daniel asking, 'How do I say my dad has cancer?'

Then we all splintered to different rooms in the house. It was shuttle sobbing. Me with Lowri, Caroline with Daniel, me with Daniel and Caroline with Lowri. It turned out that Lowri had guessed, because she had seen a text come through on Caroline's iPad, so the poor kid had been living with a kaleidoscope of half facts for over a week. She'd carried the weight on her own and I hadn't been there to help her. Daniel seemed to feel the anger of 'why my dad?' He was also rational and focused on, 'Yes, but what if you're in the unlucky ten or fifteen percent?' I remember trying to get out all the positive messages in the script again, but using different words and trying to make the abnormal seem normal, while holding him as we cried together. We all cried some more and then I think we were all sucked down into an exhausted end-of-day sleep.

The next day Daniel had a county football match in the evening and asked me two or three times if he should get out of it. I completely misread him and in the spirit of 'Of course, life goes on', gently pushed him to carry on. Maybe I thought it would help and maybe I simply got it wrong, given that I wasn't exactly on solid ground myself.

It was a cold, foggy night at a typical market-town football club under floodlights, with stone terraces surrounded by car parks on one side and waste ground on the others. The spectators were dads and brothers, all breathing fog and hot chocolate into the night air, while the players warmed up and took last-minute instructions. I'd spent the hour before kick-off calling close friends and keeping pretty well to script. Everyone had been great and hadn't made it a drama but, in a bloke kind of way, I felt loved all the same. Going to watch the game, I was feeling buoyant and upbeat.

For the first half, it was normal stuff, though the standard of football was a step above the usual Sunday morning games. Daniel, as goalkeeper, was playing pretty well, though I was aware that he kept looking over at me. I'd been talking about generalities to a couple of dads that I knew, but was blissfully unaware of what was going on in Daniel's head. I'd had three weeks to absorb the situation, but for him it was a raw twenty-four hours only. Half-time came, and I watched them emerge from the mist and cold to walk down the tunnel and into the changing room. They were back out fifteen minutes later for the second half, and immediately my subconscious knew something wasn't right. We had only ten and no keeper. Deep down, I knew it wasn't as simple as he'd gone back for his gloves. My legs moved faster than my brain and I started to walk, then run to the tunnel. The coach said something I didn't take in and pointed to the home changing room. As I walked in, my beautiful boy was sitting hunched and desolate, with his oversized gloves hanging down lifelessly between his legs. He was softly crying and couldn't say anything through the confusion. I just had to get him out of there without having to run the gauntlet of well-meaning dads in the stand. We were sitting at the back of the bar when the coach found us. I think he told us to go or maybe I told him we were going but we had to get back to the safety of the car. Then I went back to explain to the other dads which, inadvertently, proved to be an important thing to have done – the next day Daniel got many messages from his mates who demonstrated maturity way beyond what I'd expect from fifteen-year-olds. He was saved from having to put it into words himself.

I do know that we talked properly on the way home. I know we talked about death. I know we talked about how proud we were of each other and I know we talked about how shit can happen. I don't think we talked properly for a long time after that, but it was good at the time and maybe it hadn't been such a mistake to go to the match.

I still had other people to tell and I was especially worried about my family. But I had the task first of telling my Croydon mates and especially my long-term mate and business partner Robin. We'd been through his brain tumour the year before, so this wasn't going to be a 'script conversation'. It went something like this: 'You know the brain tumour you had last year?... And you know it wasn't malignant?... Well, you're a fucking lightweight, because I've got one, and it's a proper cancer this time'. There were a few moments of silence, then, 'No! You wanker, you wanker.' Strange as it sounds, it was a really touching response.

I also needed to tell my parents and sisters but I'd no idea how to go about it, so I had put it off too long – no parent should hear this message from their child and I pray I never have to. But in the end, it went well. There were lots of tears and reassurance from my sisters and a gentle, deep-felt concern from my dad, who took a well-earned break from being our rock. My mother, whom I had been most worried about, was obviously upset but chose to focus on the medical facts; maybe her own experience of breast cancer had given her the perspective and strength to identify and concentrate on what was important.

Looking back, it's a demonstration of how much responsibility we take for our impact on others. This isn't to the exclusion of our own fears but it does foster a sense of purpose, a caring purpose that maybe helps give perspective and, at its simplest, shifts the focus onto worrying about someone else.

And I was one of the lucky ones.

That weekend, or maybe the next weekend, we had a small party with fifteen or sixteen good friends. We played a game of Cancer Top Trumps and I only came third, behind a double mastectomy and a rare form of stomach cancer. Robin had to throw in his hernia, alongside his brain tumour, to even scrape fourth. Someone said that having cancer may be a bastard, but you do get to realise how much you are loved. It was a very special night that I will never forget.

Cancer: the Treatment

Someone once told me that most cancers can be cured, but that the treatment necessary to achieve this would be physically intolerable in many cases. The adverse effects would be just too devastating and the body wouldn't be able to handle it. I'm hugely grateful that my cancer was, hopefully, fixable, but I was given a harsh lesson in how brutal the treatment can be – and mine was by no means the worst that people have to suffer... I'm one of the lucky ones.

I like to think my doctors took a view that I was strong enough and young enough that they could throw the kitchen sink at me, but maybe that is just a natural desire to be a bit special – or have an edge over this horrible disease. Whatever... they did throw the kitchen sink at me. I was to have six weeks of radiotherapy, five days a week, top-and-tailed with two doses of chemotherapy. I was warned that there would be little impact at the start, but that it would get materially worse around weeks three to five – then tail off slowly over weeks six to ten. My experience was shit from day one and continued that way through to about week eleven or twelve, followed by a gradual, but by no means linear, recovery over at least twelve months.

Before it all kicked off, I had to see the oral surgeon to have a potentially infected wisdom tooth out as a precaution, given where the radiotherapy was going to be aimed. It was half an hour of hell, including eight failed injections, and it culminated in her effectively sitting on me, yanking out the broken bits of my stubborn tooth while I yelled and squirmed. I think she felt as bad about it as I did but, in the spirit of black humour, she told me that I had almost certainly emptied her waiting room.

The first stage of this particular cancer treatment is that you get a mask made – it's like something out of *The Matrix* and is as good a representation of your face, neck and shoulders as you are ever likely to have. It's used to clip you on to a hard bed or trolley so that you can be zapped in exactly the right place. Presumably, there is a complex algorithm behind it all, but for me it was just a testament to the brilliance of the doctors and staff who made the whole thing happen. It kept me still for fifteen or twenty minutes a session, making sure the tumour wasn't a moving target. I tried to come up with a name for the mask, as others apparently do, but in the end, it was all too scary for that.

Next came the first night of chemo. Caroline stayed with me in the early evening and it was all fairly relaxed. I had one of my worst ever meals – hospital-prepared curry and chips – but, overall, I was pretty buoyant. We'd discussed the treatment and I'd thought about it so often that it was becoming part of me: exemplifying the powerful human ability to coat a problem in a protective shell.

After Caroline left, I read and watched television, before tempting the god of hubris by sending a text to Robin saying I didn't know why he had made such a fuss over his brain tumour. Three hours later, I was crawling out of the room on my hands and knees, looking for a nurse and feeling sicker than I can ever remember feeling in my life. When you have chemo, the product comes in an ice-cold, grey bag, covering up its horrible toxic nature. The first time, you don't recognise it as a silent poisoner; the next time, even the look of it creates a heaving reaction in the body... And I'm one of the lucky ones.

The next morning in the hospital was my second radiotherapy session and I somehow made it downstairs for my appointment. Despite all the anti-nausea drugs I'd been given, I felt as sick as a dog and I was especially worried about throwing up in the mask. I figured choking to death on my own vomit while strapped into a facsimile of myself would be just too surreal.

The daily treatment was at the Royal Marsden where I quickly became institutionalised and enveloped in its deeply caring, professional efficiency. Despite the fact that I was fine to drive, Caroline insisted on taking me to start with, before passing the baton to two great friends who organised some sort of rota to take me in each day. I called them my 'carers' and I'm grateful for the bollocks we talked and the gallows humour we indulged in. People called and emailed as well and, by some sort of silent agreement, our interactions were honest and unsentimental.

I don't think I completely got over the sick feeling from the chemo, but the radiotherapy was pretty low impact for the first couple of weeks – though I started to go off my food fairly early on. And then, suddenly, I completely lost my appetite. I couldn't get anything solid past my mouth without gagging, and even the thought of eating made me feel sick. I was on Greek yogurt liquidised with some fruit, two different flavours of Complan and, on a good day, maybe one Weetabix, soaked in milk. The pressure was on to take in around two thousand calories a day, with the very real threat of having to have a tube stuck in my stomach if I lost too much weight. I weighed myself, and was weighed, regularly and the whole thing became like trying to slow down a ball as it accelerated downhill. I had to eat but it was disgusting and I had to face every day knowing I had to force food down me simply to function. I couldn't eat with the family because of the smell and I became increasingly isolated as my identity as a patient overrode my identity as a parent, a husband and an emotionally engaged human being. In short, I felt very sorry for myself and was often unable to rise above a miasma of desperation. I could cajole myself with the logic of 'it's only six more weeks' and 'it's only milk-type stuff' but it just felt like too long a road. There were too many days ahead to take it one day at a time. On top of all this, I was now on a cocktail of painkillers and anti-nausea tablets which really screwed my stomach, making eating even more difficult.

Throughout this whole process, the most acute lesson is that you are dealing with life stripped of all adornments. You have to eat to live, you have to deal with existential fear, you have to experience the pain, you are a parent who has hurt and frightened your children and you know that your family and friends love you unconditionally. It's all unbelievably raw but it's not all bad, because you see yourself in your truly vulnerable state and you know that there is some inner resilience there – not all the time, but it's there. The awareness of this vulnerability and resilience is profound, it's deep, and it can educate or stimulate you, while simultaneously numbing you back to the womb.

I've been fortunate enough to live my life in a relatively healthy, first-world environment, where most of my medical issues have been self-inflicted rugby wounds or minor injuries. But hospitals are eco-systems in their own right, which you only experience when you are thrown properly into the system. It's a curious mixture of organisation and chaos, laced throughout with care and honesty. I'm hugely grateful to my two consultants, to the nutrition team, to the admin team, to the radiotherapy team, to the nurses and clinical experts. I'm also grateful to my fellow patients who formed a disparate, floating tribe: the oncology consultant who had also developed cancer; the permanently cheerful guy with prostate cancer; the old guy who had to stand because of his various drips; even those who just wanted to stare at their feet lost in their own thoughts – they were all important to me, though I never knew their names. We were all there having to deal with our own crises, but were sharing a deep vulnerability.

I was also lucky to have a friend of a friend, Joe, who was six or seven weeks ahead of me in the treatment cycle and for almost exactly the same problem. He talked to me a few times and was someone to text occasionally when the going got too tough. He was a complete stranger but just having him there and sharing the experiences made it a bit easier.

I got to the end of week six, and I was still hardly able to eat and feeling pretty rough. I needed to see when it was going to end. I don't think I had expected to be skipping down Sloane Street at the end of the treatment but, in my mind, I was clearly going to be back on the road to recovery. And I wasn't, which made me want to cry in frustration. For the kind of person who needs to plan and have goals or time-frames, this was doubly hard. I felt I was due a break.

I'd lost ten kilos or about ten percent of my starting weight and it was gathering pace. I'd lost a lot of muscle and the gods, as they are wont to do, had left me with a gut and what looked like an old man's arse. I had really unpleasant burns on the side of my face and most food still made me gag. As a small victory, I found that I could eat tiny amounts of white bread, so I spent hours tearing pieces off, dipping them in butter and forcing them down. I was immensely proud of myself for this.

During this period, I had the first of two scans to assess how successful we had been. All the fears were building back again, even though, objectively, it looked like I was doing well. As we got in the car to go to the consultant's office, I received a text from him, for which I will be eternally grateful. It said, simply, 'Scan is perfect. See you later,' and we drove down the A40 in a *Chitty Chitty Bang Bang* car.

About ten weeks in, I went down to Swansea to see my family, partly because I needed to get away, and partly to give Caroline and the kids a break from me. No one ever says as much, but it must be very hard for your immediate family to live with the downer of your sickness, day-in-day-out. It was especially challenging as both kids were full-on with GCSEs and A-Levels.

The visit to Swansea constituted something of a turning point, prompted by meeting one of my sisters in a casual restaurant. I don't know if she set it up deliberately, but I forced myself away from the fortified drinks on which I had been subsisting, and ate half a rubbishy pizza and drank a beer. I had a second beer that made me feel really sick again, but the seal had been broken and I felt that I was on the road back to normal eating.

Then, came the next scan, looking for new secondaries – the bogeyman word in cancer. Foolishly, I went alone, and I hadn't had the magic text from the consultant, so this time it felt like driving a Chiefdom Tank down the A40. As I arrived, and was frigging around with the parking machine, I got a call from my consultant's PA to say the scan was clear. Taking the call, I was rudely holding up another man at the machine, but he must have sensed my relief and emotion, and generously waved my apologies away.

I went to the consultation armed with my usual list of oddball questions. What I really wanted to know was how often I would be scanned in the future, but I was shocked by the answer, which was something like: 'You won't be, because if you have a secondary in this form, you probably don't want to know. We won't be able to cure it and it will be all about palliative care – so the longer you are unaware and enjoying life, the better.' Or, to view it another way, if this scan had been bad, we would have been having a conversation about how much time I had left. It was searing in its honesty, and I came to appreciate and be grateful for it, but, at the time, I felt like I'd been walking in the fog without realising how close I was to a sheer cliff face... And I'm one of the lucky ones.

The second all-clear had been a big step, though I found myself developing a language to protect myself against fate when talking to others – 'It's hopefully all okay'; 'I'm fine at the moment but I'll be continually tested and poked about'; 'So far, so good'. Life was starting to take over, and I had to manage my depleted energy levels against the positive impulse of trying to get back to normal. This was a problem, partly because, psychologically, I was not on solid ground and partly because it's not a linear process. The effects of the treatment can hit you hard from nowhere and also give you days of almost complete normality. This, and the inevitability of ageing, is a balance that I had to struggle with for a couple of years post-treatment.

My first mistake was to go to a business meeting in the States. It entailed four days of jet lag, continual meetings and evenings of entertaining or socialising. When I got back, I was wrecked and spent most of the next ten days in bed or wandering in and out of business or family issues. On top of this, I was angry with myself for overdoing it, and cross with the disease for not letting me be myself. As it turned out, I was not half as cross and angry as Caroline was, because I'd made myself sick again and potentially ruined a big family holiday. We were due to fly to Boston two weeks after my return from the US, but the night before I had real doubts if I could even make it through the airport. Somehow, though, I did, and I thanked God that I'd used my air miles to book business class flights, or it would have been a hellish trip. Even then, I couldn't make it out with the family for dinner that night and I distinctly remember the feeling of sad isolation, stuck alone with only CNN for company. New England was great, though, and soon I was able to walk decent distances and even paddleboard on the sea. We drove and travelled around, eating in various restaurants despite my weird appetite. For some bizarre reason, I found I could eat vast quantities of clam chowder, which became my staple for the holiday.

Although I enjoyed the trip, it was characterised by occasional big arguments with the kids. One of the side-effects of treatment and recovery is that you effectively put on hold your parenting responsibilities. They were pussy-footing around me, while I hadn't got the energy to fight them on certain things. By the time we got to Boston, they were also four months more mature, multiplied by a factor of four for having to watch their dad being very sick. So, they had moved on and I wasn't able to randomly drop back into parenting at the point where I'd left it four months previously. The arguments were horrible and very upsetting for everyone. Maybe they were understandable, as there was a pressure pumped up to a scale of magnitude greater than any normal parent-teenager relationship. It made me really wary of conflict, but it also brought it home how much they had been bottling up. Neither of the kids was good at articulating their emotions, but they were just hurting, frightened and angry – and I'd caused that. I had to learn to take a step back and not react when there were inexplicable tensions, effectively ceding some parental power to help salve the wounds.

After the holiday, I needed to commit more to my work, which had fortunately been doing okay, despite my erratic engagement. Gradually, my energy was returning, although I learned to avoid international travel or back-to-back big days. I'd say that six months from the end of treatment I was ninety percent back in action, and a hundred percent on a good day if I didn't push it.

Physically, I could also feel myself getting stronger now that I was six months in. I did much more walking as well as mountain bike bursts. On the last day before the treatment started, I'd done my bike course in forty-seven minutes. Ten months later, I was achieving around fifty-three minutes and getting better every time. Twelve months later, I did forty-six and cried big, blobby tears coming into the driveway. The boys' trip in November to walk a section of the South Downs Way was also a critical milestone. Now I could do a hard day and survive far too many beers in the evening as well. I started playing tennis again, in addition to doing some proper weights to build back some of the lost muscle. The muscle recovery was a struggle, not least because I wilfully get older each year, but it's all part of getting back to normal.

It's the emotional side that is most significant. As humans, of course, we live with the concept of our death from a relatively early age. However, if you are lucky enough to be fit and healthy, death in itself, and particularly your own, is an abstract concept. When you get very sick, it becomes glaringly real. We are forced to face the fact that we might not be around for much longer. Everything we have learned, experienced and looked forward to disappears. We will be no more, except in the memory of, maybe, three generations of loved ones. There are existential questions like: has my life been worthwhile? Have I wasted or used my time well? What, if anything, happens next?

I don't particularly have a faith to fall back on and, even in the darker times, I didn't want to go down that path. Maybe, one day I will, but it has to be a positive realisation or choice – an epiphany, not a lifeboat. On top of this, and probably the hardest part, is the effect on your family and friends. You want to protect them from the pain and yet you want to be honest. You want to help them after you are gone, but you understand how unpredictable life can be in the future. You want to die or survive well so as not to frighten them or leave them with bad memories. All of this and more crowds your thoughts while you are trying to get back to normal... And I'm one of the lucky ones.

My chances are very good and I'm progressing well. I've been checked every month, every quarter and every six months by some of the best clinicians in the country. Yet, I still hate the day of testing. It brings it all back, front and centre, not least because having a camera stuck up your nose and down your throat is absolutely no fun. What is fun, though, is the elation when it's finished: sticky buns on Marylebone High Street and giving all my money away to the homeless on the street.

It's been an extraordinary psychological experience, on top of the rollercoaster that was the diagnosis and treatment. It has not always been a bad experience – in fact, often there have been good parts to it; it's just hard to unpick and make sense of. There are very dark nights when it comes flooding in, but there are also times of profound sensitivity and emotional insight. My relationships with friends are closer and more fulfilling. I think I'm more forgiving and engaged with Caroline and my kids, though I am by no means perfect. I haven't magically been given a new personality but some of the edges have been knocked off. I'm more attuned to the outside world: not in a clunky 'smell the roses' kind of way, but with a sharper awareness and sense of my own presence. I'm also more interested in ideas or experience. I cry more often, prompted by reading or hearing something – after nearly five years, I still can't relate the story of telling my kids without my voice breaking. I also can't help myself looking for stories about people with cancer or other health problems. There must be good reasons for this around survivor guilt, or a mental amulet for the future, but for now I just recognise it for what it is.

Probably the most interesting effect has been how it has changed my views on the short-term and long-term future. I passionately dislike the phrase 'It makes you realise what is important in life'. I understand it, and I understand that people need it as a shorthand and something to say, but it is a phrase that blots out the nuances and emotional complexity of the human condition. What cancer does is dramatically blur the edges between our conscious, or subconscious, existential awareness. It breaks down the compartmentalised, coping strategies that enable us to live day-to-day – death is no longer abstract. This is not necessarily a bad thing, but certainly it makes life less predictable and less comfortable.

I know that I want to experience more, and I now think in terms of having a finite time left, whether a year or thirty years. I don't want to waste energy and time on things that drain me, but I also need to be in the real world of work and responsibilities and where 'shit happens'. I want to prepare my kids for life but at the same time acknowledge that they must go through their own experiences and traverse their own emotional landscapes.

For me, my reaction to having cancer hasn't been a blinding flash of light that has enabled me to see all with clarity. It would be great if it were and I'm envious of those who have had a big window opened. I am just happy that I'm a bit richer, a bit wiser and that I can see more of the blurred images through some kind of window. I'm not ready to die yet and I hope it comes to me at a time when I am ready for it. I know it won't be my choice, but at least I'm a little more prepared. Meanwhile, I've decided never to turn down an invitation, though fortunately so far nobody has suggested Morris Dancing. I've got plans to do more, travel more, read more and love more. I want to laugh more, I want to be there for people, whether loved ones or strangers, and I want to be the 'Catcher in the Rye' for my children – they mustn't know about it, but I'll be the one patrolling the cliff, keeping them away from danger while they play unaware in the long grass.

I learned a lot in the first twelve months after the diagnosis. Not immutable facts, but they helped me and may help others.

- First and foremost, I have learned that I am loved.
- I've experienced deep vulnerability and been terrified out of my wits.
- I've had to hurt my kids and family and watch them survive and grow.
- I've been on the receiving end of fantastic care and I can't understand why it isn't an inalienable right for all people.
- I've seen doctors and medical professionals who know what they are doing most of the time, but who need you to contribute with your experiences. They are managing in very clever generalities, but they can't always predict how our incredibly complex physiologies or psychologies will interact. We need to tell them.

- It's better to go with a friend or loved one to see clinicians – I doubt if I took in more than half of what was said; you need someone with you to listen properly.
- Hospitals and health services are about organised chaos – this used to frustrate me but they are places for sick people, not businesses or social organisations that conform to budgets and timetables. People get sick, priorities change and damaged people walk or are carried through the door. I found it helpful to check dates or actions myself, and, if necessary, organise and manage the process.
- I resolved to give myself a break and listen to my body. In my case, this ranged from watching over a hundred episodes of *Nashville* when I needed to escape, through to pushing myself to do more exercise than I thought possible. It meant eating when I could and getting used to just not wanting to eat when it was a bad day.
- Finally, I learned that if you are lucky with your diagnosis, you do come through. Some don't, and they may well have been better people, more deserving or more willing to fight harder than me, so I don't crow about my survival. There were times when I thought I wouldn't make it, but I did, and I'm very grateful for that. In some ways, I have emerged stronger, but I wouldn't romanticise this either, as there is no way I'd choose to go through any of it again.

I also know that... I'm one of the lucky ones.

Cancer: the Epilogue

Last week, I was finally signed off, five years after my treatment for throat cancer. With hindsight, this was always going to be an important day, but I hadn't expected to be so thrown off-balance. I hadn't anticipated anything, in fact, and had viewed the appointment as a formality. I'd been going every two months to the Marsden or the clinic, then every three months and finally every six months, culminating in last Wednesday evening when my fabulous oncologist shook me by the hand and said he hoped never to see me again. By now, the appointments had become relatively routine as, after three years, you are pretty unlucky if you get any recurrence – but still I hated the build-up and would get really tetchy a couple of days before the lonely drive down the A40. I always put it down to the prospect of having that camera stuck up my nose and down my throat, which is something I wouldn't wish on anyone. Admittedly, it's only a thin lit-tube covered in gel, not your average Box Brownie, but it makes you gag on the way down and on the way back out. The experience is about forty-five seconds of misery, followed by a pat on the shoulder to say it's all looking good and it's clear.

Typically, once released, the euphoria kicked in somewhere around Marylebone High Street, but this time I had barely got out of the consultant's office before my eyes started to prick with tears and my emotions swamped me. It felt like a physical untwisting of the gut. Five years earlier, I had begged whichever god was listening to 'give me five more years' and here I was, five years later – warm and vertical, with two kids nearly through university, and feeling like a success. Somehow, I was out the other side.

Sitting in a café on the high street, the light was different and the pedestrians moved a tiny bit more slowly. The car drivers were slightly less aggressive and the waitress randomly came up and clinked my beer bottle, saying 'Cheers'. Somehow, I was slightly different, and people and the world seemed to know this. This has happened to me once or twice in life, after deeply emotional experiences, and it's the most extraordinary sensation. All my senses wanted to work together as if, at some pre-planned signal, they would transcend the everyday. I saw the things around me with absolute clarity, without trying to place them in their circumstances. In fact, I wasn't thinking at all; I was just present and grounded in where I was. Some may call it a karma or existential peace, but I don't call it anything because it's unnameable and inexplicable. To name it would be to think about something, when not thinking was what gave me that gift for a few minutes. Of course, it doesn't last and the traffic at Gypsy Corner will drag any tranquillity out of the peaceful soul, but there is a gentle, residual memory one week later and I'm trying to keep hold of it.

I wonder if I've learned something that will help me when my time comes around again. It's unlikely to be throat cancer because we've blasted the hell out of that, but it will be something, because that's the human condition. Maybe I've had my dress rehearsal and I won't be so terrified next time, though on balance, going quickly in a non-violent death still holds a lot of appeal. I reserve the right to go blubbing and unreasonably angrily into the long good night, but there is a chance that I'll be more accepting and peaceful, and maybe someone will want to chink a glass with me, and say 'Cheers'.

Ziggy

This week we have had to have our beautiful, family dog of fifteen years put down, leaving me hollowed out and profoundly sad. It's a dull, deep ache in my bones, which is liquefied in the bottom of my stomach. It's not something I can think my way through, so I have no choice but to live with it and experience the pain.

And yet the 'life and times of Ziggy' is a fabulously positive story of luck and joy. It's a story that nearly didn't happen at all, which would have robbed us of one of the most important relationships in our family's life and deprived an insecure dog of her forever home.

Ziggy, originally named Savana, was born in the Dogs' Trust Rehoming Centre at Harefield, before she was joined up with her first family. Sadly, for unknown reasons, that family was forced to bring her back to face the lottery of finding another home. Right up until the end, Ziggy couldn't bear the sight of suitcases in the hallway, and would lie across the doorway to remind us not to forget her.

She wasn't even on the list of dogs we were due to see, but a member of staff just had an instinct to put her forward, and she won us over at once. It wasn't a great beginning, as she started attacking men with beards and people on bikes – and this was especially difficult as we live near the woods with numerous cycle paths. We learned to apologise a lot and spot the signs of trouble, but we did have some very real fears that this wasn't going to work out. To reassure you, 'no bearded cyclists were hurt in the making of this film'. She did settle down and soon slipped into the role of protector of our two small children, insisting on being on guard outside their rooms, after we failed to keep her downstairs in her basket. She was loved by them and us and the love was returned unconditionally.

Dog trainers talk about finding the key motivations of your animal and for her it was a love of balls and exercise. She would run for hours after a ball, though she never developed the skill of giving it back. The rugby ball was her nemesis because it bounced unpredictably and she would bark crossly if it couldn't be hunted down easily when at full pelt. She was my running and mountain bike partner for many years and appointed herself to the water ski team, tirelessly chasing down the boat on the bank if one of us was being towed. Maybe, with hindsight, all of this exacerbated her arthritis in later life, but it's hard to imagine stopping a dog who ran for the pure joy of running. Over time, we had to drop the hard exercise but even in later life she considered it a right to walk and sniff at least for a few yards outside the house.

After the initial issues, we never really had any problems, mainly because she just wanted to be with us. She was a stoic dog who right up until the end tried not to show the pain and gamely tried to get involved. She was also discreet, if you can apply that word to a dog – she would always go off the path to go to the toilet and was scrupulously clean.

All of this made her decline so hard to witness. Her back legs started to go, so she had trouble getting up; then there was a kidney infection and finally some incontinence which, for such a fastidious animal, must have been awful – you could almost feel her embarrassment. Her hearing and eyesight got worse, but the instinct for where one of us was remained undiminished. She looked so tired sometimes, yet on other occasions would sit up, scanning the house for what was going on. Sometimes she would eat and sometimes refuse even the smallest of treats – deeply suspicious that we were trying to get tablets down her. It's a stretch to say that she knowingly spat out pills that were to help her, but she was a pain in the arse about taking any, despite our trying all sorts of expensive meats and special foods to tempt her. We happily spent a fortune on pills, hydrotherapy, acupuncture and vets' bills, but we couldn't fight nature – and at the end we didn't think she wanted to fight along with us.

Probably one of the hardest parts was that there was no event to trigger a decision – she just got slowly and almost imperceptibly worse. We knew it was coming and had hoped she would go peacefully in her sleep, but that was not the fate that was destined for Ziggy. As on many other occasions, we found we were making decisions with incomplete information, but this was a life-or-death decision, tangled up in our feelings and our sense of obligation. Should we drag it out for her and us? Should we have gone earlier? And, for me, did I have the right to end an animal's life? The answer to the last question is probably yes, and that I have a responsibility to avoid unnecessary suffering, but I was still very uncomfortable with it. In the end, and once we called the vet, everything happened very quickly, which in itself was a deeply unsettling thing. We were functioning in a slightly surreal space, moving one foot in front of the other but knowing that a shocking series of events was unfolding.

She was stressed in the car, mainly, we suspect, because she was incontinent, but she was calmer once we had arrived and we could just love her. The vet's surgery was very caring and compassionate as both Caroline and I took turns at crying. We were with her at the end, when we were able to hug and talk to her, while watching the life slip out of her. Her great big heart stopped and, though the body twitched for a minute or so longer, Ziggy had gone and only a shell was left.

Her spirit and everything that made up Ziggy was going to have to reside in our memories and in our lived experience – teaching us to love more in the future. It was shockingly final thing, and almost inexplicably quick, but seeing an empty body is part of the necessary grieving process. Writing this, four days later, I'm still not on solid ground, except I know I've been sad and upset and exposed to the rawness of deep emotions. We now come home to a house without her presence and her life force, and only a visceral feeling of loss as we walk through the door. First thing in the morning we don't have to let her out and give her breakfast. Then at five in the evening she isn't padding around, making sure we haven't forgotten dinner. Things that used to be a chore we now miss, each time jolting us back to when she was just there and part of us. I wish we still had those chores.

I make no comparisons with other profound human emotions, but I'm looking back on the life of a loved family pet, the rawness of how I feel having lost her and the impact that she has had on my life: She taught me about my need to nurture; she showed the value of purely being herself without artifice; and she reflected the experience of unthinking joy that makes us richer and more emotionally complete people. Throughout history, people have had powerful relationship with dogs, even back to prehistoric humans who were often buried with their animals. Maybe it's a mutual reliance: getting through the practicalities of life with a working dog. Maybe it's our need to be responsible for another being. Maybe it's the unconditional, no-strings-attached love that is a step removed from conditional human love. Maybe it's the vulnerability of something that is dependent on us for food and warmth that reminds us of our own responsibilities as people. Whatever it is, my family and I have been lucky and privileged with Ziggy and I need to say it out loud.

Heaven Can Wait

As part of my naked attempt to get into God's good books, I sometimes drive older people to hospital appointments, though I think I probably get more out of the experience than they do. In part, I'm drawn in because of my sensitivity to any health diagnosis after my own brush with cancer and, in part, because other people's stories can often be life-affirming. Plus, there is the pleasure of joining a community enterprise where so many contribute for the good of others. I've learned a lot from the company of these clear-thinking and interesting older people, who should still have agency in our society. I'd like to share just two examples.

One lady is notable just because of the shit she has to handle and how she goes about doing it. Firstly, my sat nav couldn't find her address so I stopped in the local pub to ask. The landlord knew the road and certainly knew the lady, although she hadn't been there for years and was a non-drinker. Clearly a local character. When I finally reached her front door, she came out using a walking frame, joking with neighbours about having her booster jab in her bum. Her knee was so bad and painful that if she didn't use a walking frame, it was a wheelchair, yet she'd been unable to get a proper date for a simple operation to fix the problem. Then it turned out that her husband was coming home from hospital, having been recently diagnosed with incurable cancer, and given a couple of weeks to live. As we talked, the conversation crystallised around her fears of not being able to look after him properly, and what she should do if her possible knee operation was confirmed in the time he had left. Older people have so many barriers when dealing with a health service that wants you to 'go online' or 'download an app'– it makes me very cross on their behalf, although she herself wasn't especially angry about it. At no point did she complain about her circumstances, her luck or the health service – it was what it was. The situation was hopeless, yet she was not helpless, and there was clearly an impressive life-force keeping her strong.

Another lady, with the poise and elegance of someone who knows themselves well, shared that her husband had, some years previously, been diagnosed with a serious heart weakness, with a prognosis that it would give out in the next ten to fifteen years. They had resolved not to talk about it again and just kind of went for life – travelling, meeting friends and family and enjoying what for both of them was a second marriage. She loved to cook and his favourite hobby was eating whatever she cooked – especially roast dinners. She softly recalled a Sunday morning, preparing a joint of lamb, while chatting through the open door, surrounded by the smells of meat fat and roasting potatoes. But halfway through the conversation, he stopped answering. He was peacefully sitting upright in his chair and his heart had just stopped – and that is how she found him. Years later, she was proudly happy that his last experience was of her cooking his favourite roast dinner.

Tribal Man

As much as I enjoy the community and camaraderie of being part of a tribe, I am aware that, taken to excess, it can be a dangerous and insidious thing. Tribalism is the outcome of an unregulated need to belong, allied with the inability of the rational to override the irrational. It operates in four ways: firstly, it addresses a desperate and innate need to avoid a Hobbesian state of nature that is 'solitary, poor, nasty, brutish and short'; it also satisfies a psychological need to join a club or tribe and adhere to its rules, however malignant; thirdly, it feeds our desire to see ourselves as superior to others; and fourthly, it legitimises our wish to impose our rules on others whom we believe to be inferior or a threat. We want to look similar, sound similar and come from a similar part of the world – because it's either safer, more nurturing or more successful. Of course, I'm not immune: I can support England at rugby against another Home Nations team, then seamlessly switch allegiances to the British and Irish Lions against a very different tribe from the southern hemisphere. I can believe that my tribe is better than another tribe and celebrate the differences and I'm pretty sure that if my tribe was threatened, I'd join in the fight. What I hope I wouldn't do is to contribute to forcing the will of my tribe on other tribes.

I'm forced to recognise that labels are good shortcuts to understanding individuals or peoples. It saves having to think too hard about the complex individual in front of me. If they are white, English, a parent or a particular age I can make certain assumptions – and I may have to do this many times a day. If they have a similar set of characteristics to me, I feel more comfortable. My tribe, like others, will incorporate the good, the bad, the boring, the frustrating and the downright scary – and all of these will all shelter under the one umbrella, so I have to give them more respect than they may deserve. In addition, I could miss the brilliance of people and values in the other tribe, because I'm devoting my emotional energy to the mediocre in my own. From the banal to the brutal, tribalism is manifest in our collective psychology – and I see it wherever I look.

I see it in sport, where an Arsenal supporter, for example, is differentiated from a Man United fan. Drilling down further, perhaps an Arsenal supporter who sits in the Clock End sees himself as different from the North End guy; maybe an old Highbury season ticket holder feels different from an upstart, Emirates only, season ticket holder. I have an extraordinary image in my mind from a recent game – grown men with bulging necks and eyes, screaming, challenging and gesturing to opposition supporters a hundred metres away, but from the safety of their block. Meanwhile, the game – that they, and we, had paid to see – continued. My cohort will support Team GB in the Olympics and passionately support England against Scotland in the Euros – and even root for Bourne End Junior Sports Club Under-11s against the nemesis that is Chesham Under-11s.

I see it in work, where the positioning of your company or institution in relation to another requires constant attention.

Within organisations you could be part of an acquired business which feels either special or persecuted. You could be in a department that feels itself to be a shining star in the midst of mediocrity, or you could have been through some significant shared experience that will always connect you to the team: 'Remember when we...?' Sometimes, because of this, poor decisions are made and resources are misused.

I see it in families, where jokes about in-laws are at one end of a spectrum that ends with feuds that can run through generations. Are you more like your father's side or more like your mother's side? Who do you identify with most? Who do you align with in a fight or argument? What happens when marriage breakdowns occur, with fights over custody or the splitting of assets? In the name of this, people have been made very unhappy, alienated or desperately lonely.

I see it in nationalism, where we pit our English qualities, against those of, say, the French. On home turf, we are even further divided. Maybe we see ourselves as tough, plain-speaking northerners or as sophisticated southerners. Possibly we think of ourselves as young, liberal-minded millennials, or as traditional protectors of the best of society. We may see ourselves as a Mancunian or a Liverpudlian and anyone in between as a 'Woolyback'. Any ethnic or religious group denied a fair chance at life's opportunities will fight back with violence. We only have to look to Northern Ireland to see evidence of this at a national level. At its most extreme, people support or turn a blind eye to the organised death of millions of other human beings, destroying communities and eradicating histories. In the 1994 Rwandan genocide, the world looked away as even neighbours turned against each other. Ethnic cleansing is an appalling euphemism in our modern lexicon. Its reach extends from the unthinkably vicious to the subtly coercive. In its name, throughout history, many millions of people have been brutally killed or displaced.

I see it in religion, where beliefs can often be fundamentally opposed, from Buddhism to Christianity, from Judaism to Islam, and where there are also differences within each religion. We may be on the Catholic wing of the Christian Church or we may be on the Protestant wing – passionately disagreeing under one broad ideology. We may be Protestant, but devoutly Baptist or strongly Methodist – with almost infinite variations and identities within each. Religion has an appalling history of exclusion, violence and persecution, which is not consigned to the past. People are still being seriously disadvantaged in life chances, forced to deny their faith or killed for their beliefs.

I see it in international relations, where countries are always jostling for position. Are we in the club of democratic nations and do we jealously guard our place on the Security Council, the ultimate big boys' club? Or are we a non-conformist state like Venezuela or Cuba who, for self-protection, side with the powerful non-conformist state of Russia? And who defines a state? The answer is the most powerful group, or the group who got there first. The winners will divide countries, cutting across ethnic and religious groups and not always for bad reasons – maybe for the lesser of the evils? These winners will quickly form transnational groups – either for protection, like NATO; economic wellbeing, like the EU; or ideological colonialism, like the Warsaw Pact. And, again, this is not just consigned to the past – where will the minorities in Crimea and Ukraine end up? Indeed, how will we manage a border in Northern Ireland?

Tribes form and reform, potentially cutting across other tribal groups – whether you are Conservative or Labour, you could be a Remainer or a Brexiteer with allegiances pulled in many directions, eclipsing the core political ideology. You may be labelled a racist, a little Englander or a wishy-washy internationalist, however well or badly you have thought through and researched your subject. In the USA, you could be a gun-control advocate or a second amendment supporter, while being a Democrat or Republican, young or old, urban or red-neck. And, of course, allegiances change, reform or wither in a state of dynamic flux. Sometimes, because of this, good alliances can be undermined or resentment is planted in people's hearts.

I see tribal allegiances challenge my own country, or the rock that I happen to live on. It's real and urgent. How will our national loyalties play out? Will Scotland, as current opinion polls suggest, break away from the union? In the Good Friday Agreement, there are provisions for a vote on a United Ireland, should the desire demonstrably be there – what will that mean for the two religious communities against the backdrop of the Troubles? And as for Wales, which is not yet minded to secede, despite its national pride, will it want to be the junior partner in a union of two? 'Britishness' as a concept is declining in favour, with 'Englishness' emerging as a counterbalancing force in England, although not as strongly as the specific national tendencies of the others' home unions. Then there is the idea of the European Union that has, as shown in many studies, failed to create emotional attachment compared to national loyalties – but is still a potentially safe economic and security harbour for small nations. Maybe the break-up of the United Kingdom will be good for people on my rock, but there will be physical or intellectual conflict where large constituencies will be, at best, disappointed or, at worst, significantly disadvantaged.

In academia, psychologists pore over tribalism and its various categories, trying to understand our fundamental social behaviour – individually and in groups. They broadly agree that some form of tribalism is inherent in man; at least, if we crawled out of the primordial swamp without it, we sure adopted it pretty quickly. Developmental psychologists explore the movement of an infant from 'it's all about me' to an understanding that there are other independent versions of 'me', through to the shocking realisation that these other 'me's are, in fact, different in their otherness, and that that is an existential threat, or at least a bit of a worry. Clearly, most of us evolve to accept and, hopefully, embrace 'otherness' but the time of complete safety is gone. Man is hard-wired to seek groups for protection and enhancement and the closer to 'me' others are, in looks, geography, values and objectives, the safer I feel. The image of a primitive tribal group fighting for scarce resources runs deep in our collective psyche but tribes can also collaborate for mutual gain – we can join together to hunt better, breed better or build organisations like NATO. Groups change and tribal allegiances change; it could be a new leader, new hunting grounds or the collapse of the Warsaw Pact that causes the previously dominant authority to implode. The manifestation of changing allegiances is extraordinarily nuanced and complex, constantly shifting, often with competing and simultaneous dynamics, and subject to difficult-to-predict internal and external pressures. Whatever the challenges, it's clear that it is a fundamental part of all societies and, simply put, a part of human nature.

George Orwell, in his seminal 1945 essay *Notes on Nationalism*, usefully interrogates the concept and how it manifests itself. Although it was written in an extraordinary political period, after the Second World War, much of his thinking stands the test of time. He makes an important distinction between patriotism and nationalism which informs the debate going on in my head. According to Orwell, patriotism is based around 'devotion to a particular place and a particular way of life'. It is a positive and defensive mindset without the desire to impose on others. Nationalism, on the other hand, is an offensive, more aggressive mindset, promoting the advancement of one nation at the expense of others... 'to secure more power and prestige, not for himself but for the unit in which he has chosen to sink his own individuality'. In addition, a softer definition of nationalism bumps into sovereignty in its desire for self-determination and the protection of its right to rule within a given territory. It recognises Rousseau's 'social contract' where a people consents to be ruled, usually within a nation-state, thereby reinforcing tribal ownership. Sovereignty has internal pressures to maintain the consent of the tribe and external pressures to control outcomes in a porous, global and inter-connected world.

Tribalism emerges from Orwell's definitions as a way of operating in the world, while ideology or philosophy are external human constructs – for example, articulating political, economic or spiritual belief systems. I might argue that tribalism is in our nature, while ideology seeks to make sense of the world that tribal man has built. Tribalism must also influence other areas where the fundamental human need-to-belong meets a man-made construct, including organised religion, political doctrines, pacifism, and more modern identity groups like Black Lives Matter or LGBTQ pressure groups. It will force us to question whether our adherence to an idea is pure, or if is there an element of 'I want to be special, because I'm in a special group'. To make the subject even more complicated, we overlay globalisation or the 'citizen of nowhere' argument, as a counterweight to our embedded tribal behaviour. The forces of the modern world pull us away from our roots or, at least, they try to. Some will take a more individualistic, international approach but, as yet, I see no evidence that our need for local or national allegiances will diminish.

Tribal labels help us define friends and enemies but they lead to dramatic simplification at best, and demonisation of other groups at worst. One of the human characteristics identified by social psychologists is the extent to which members of a group distort their rational thinking, consciously or unconsciously, to secure their place in the group. Interestingly, research has shown that there is little difference between the left and right of politics in our need to belong. Tribalism manifests a deep human conflict between our rational brain and our emotional heart, which leaves us vulnerable to exploitation by those who aspire to leadership and influence. Famously, the Brexit campaign based on redirecting £350 million each week sent to the EU was clearly a distortion of the truth, but it was designed by clever people and believed by many voters. We had the labels of 'Remainer' or 'Brexiteer' saving the population the job of thinking through a highly complex, economic, political and historic decision. Whatever your biases, and I am conflicted here, it's a lousy way of making such an important decision.

This brings us to the role of leaders. Understanding how the human need to belong is exacerbated in times of existential, economic or political stress, enables leaders to manipulate whole populations. They do this by presenting a compelling vision of the future or articulating a meaningful threat. They corral society's élites and co-opt the institutions of power; and they can inspire national pride. Churchill, for example, was able to mobilise the entire nation to fight and eventually win the Second World War, despite very difficult odds. The role of propaganda, misinformation and the deliberate distortion of the characterisation of the Germans powerfully combined to call our nation to arms. It was fundamentally a defensive rather than expansionist fight, though Britain was not without a history of conquest.

On the other hand, Hitler was able to transform a culturally sophisticated nation into an expansionist, warmongering country that ultimately tolerated the extermination of more than six million people. He used German national pride, the shame of the Versailles Treaty and the positive ideology of 'living space' to mobilise the population. Hannah Arendt famously coined the phrase 'the banality of evil' at the Eichmann trial where she highlighted how ordinary people could do everyday tasks that contributed to the most appalling outcomes. Some of these people were knowingly evil, but many were manipulated and part of a tribe careering to disaster. Complex studies of personality traits have identified that 'authoritarian bias' exists in the general population, in people who are typically obedient to authority, adhere to rules and show hostility to those who are different. These are ideal personality types to be manipulated by malevolent leaders. Interestingly, in studies trying to explain the rise of Fascism in Nazi Germany, there was no increased preponderance of this character type in mid-twentieth-century Germany versus other western countries (McAvoy, 2012). Personality types had a role to play but it was a tinderbox of complex issues, ignited by the blaze of tribalism, that ultimately sent the world up in flames.

We naturally look for safety and fulfilment in our groups,

especially when we are threatened or badly led. We have seen dreadful separatist wars in the Balkans, genocide in Rwanda and Cambodia, real and metaphorical walls between Mexico and the most powerful nation on earth; we have witnessed the Taliban's ruthless coup in Afghanistan, and the devastating war between Israel and Palestine. These conflicts all have, at their heart, nationalism, patriotism, religion or tribalism. On top of this we inhabit an internet- and social media-led world, where prejudice can be easily stoked, with very little control over fact and authenticity, and where echo chambers, blocking out debate or alternative views, are easily formed. Tribalism is a fact of life; it's whether we choose to understand it and control it for good that is the question.

One interesting sidebar to any discussion on human tribalism is its manifestation between the sexes. There is precious little academic study on the subject so I'm forced to rely on observation and instinct. I believe that women are significantly less tribal than men. Maybe they are less driven to belong or be possessed, or maybe they are less likely to subscribe to the more aggressive forms of tribalism. Football crowds tend to reflect male competitiveness, though the desire to win and enjoy winning seems to be a joint venture between the sexes – it's just I've never seen a woman facing away from the pitch for ninety minutes, making obscene hand gestures at the opposition. Maybe, given the chance, throughout history there would have been more female warlords, but I doubt it. Outward aggression is more of a male trait, while the need to protect is more of a female tendency, though both varieties of tribalism can be equally passionate and committed. The image of mothers sending their boys to war is still seared into our collective psyche, not least because of the deep maternal conflict that it represents; it's an anguish surely also experienced by fathers, but that does not feature as part of the national wartime narrative.

I started this essay with a deep distrust of tribalism, but maybe that has softened a little as I've gone through the thought process. I can reflect on some very positive elements of tribalism from the existential through to the trivial. If my British tribe had not come together to protect ourselves during a thirty year span, we could have twice been invaded and subjugated by an aggressive German state. History tells us that the victors rarely treat the vanquished as equals. I can also see positives in patriotism as defined by Orwell. Why not be proud of my group because it grounds my psychological need, making me more complete? Patriotism can just be about fun, enjoying the company of friends while supporting your country in all sorts of endeavours – from sport through to, God help us, the Eurovision Song Contest. From small groups of cavemen through to the modern nation state, we feel safer if we are similar to our fellow citizens. Yet there is a price to pay for safety.

That price is the lost opportunities and risks that tribalism brings to our world. Lost opportunities because, by taking a line of least resistance, we miss diversity and qualities in others that could enrich us. We fail to appreciate how what we choose to see in others distorts our perceptions, possibly making us do stupid, lazy or evil things. Risks because tribalism is too volatile a concept and too open to abuse by malevolent leaders. Tribalism is part of a mix, including history, economics, geography, religion and politics, which causes hurt to many people. The scary thing is how quickly we, and society as a whole, can be dragged down to the negative side of it. I'm pretty sure that if my family and friends were starving or under threat, I'd break the law and do whatever I needed to do to stop it – maybe even attack first before the threat became a reality. This is a microcosm of larger societal or ethnic group behaviour and here we are only talking about defensive tribalism. Offensive tribalism, or its manifestation in nationalism, can be extraordinarily destructive, which in turn provokes defensive tribalism as the oppressed fight for existence. And, once again, people and peoples get badly hurt.

What to do about it is especially difficult as it goes to the core of what we are. It's so embedded in our makeup that to rail against it would be pointless. It's a political issue but it's also a moral issue – and morality and politics can be taught. Education is an easy answer to lean on but it runs the risk of tokenism. Tribalism is such a huge change agent that it deserves proper scrutiny. History, economics and politics are studied because of their impact on our world, but our tribal behaviour is rarely emphasised outside of pure psychological study. If it's not a standalone subject then it needs to be a meaningful subset of the other three. To better understand our world, and our impact on it, can only be a good thing and should mean fewer of our fellow humans get hurt.

Politics: Left! Right! Left! Right! Left...?

At its most basic level, national politics can be boiled down to two things, together with our individual and collective attitude towards them. Of course, there are huge complexities in the subject but they only represent stars spinning around the two planets of economic efficiency and social equality. What is the best way to grow and improve society's wealth and what is the fairest way to distribute this wealth? Efficiency and equality are often seen, and with good reason, as mutually exclusive. These choices reflect core human attitudes and behaviours: our way of looking at the world. Our responses are not right or wrong, and motivations can be good on both sides of the debate, but understanding the core dynamics should help us when constructing a society that is more comfortable in its own skin.

My interest in politics, theoretical rather than the grubby hands-on type, has been with me all my adult life and has been bookended by two significant periods of academic study. Politics is fascinating because it shows how groups of people move and change allegiances with different circumstances and different rhetorical leadership. Ideas and arguments sway the herd, sometimes to a slight change of direction, sometimes to splinter off and sometimes to completely change course and head towards a different watering hole. However, we are not wildebeest but sophisticated animals who can think and make decisions, although the pack mentality still influences us and directs us to make decisions we might not make on our own. Maybe, because we have such busy daily lives, we tend to outsource our thinking to those at the front of the herd in the hope that they are not leading us into danger. Politics would seem be a game of leaders and followers with only crisis points or elections changing this dynamic.

Growing up in the 1970s, I had no choice but to experience the mess that we had made of our society. I don't remember having any great political affiliations, or indeed insight; I just lived through the three-day week, power cuts and the telly turning off at ten o'clock – rather quaintly – with the National Anthem. We had IRA bombings, our own civil war, and a whole series of strikes, which had little effect on me except hearing grown-ups tut a lot.

Then came Margaret Thatcher, and politics seemed to be playing by very different rules. It was about the individual and the freedom to drive economic wealth at all costs. I discovered what ideology was, though it couldn't compensate for my utter frustration at petrol prices sky-rocketing and not being able to afford to drive to my girlfriend's house – I didn't make terribly thoughtful political judgements at that age. I voted for Thatcher a couple of times; then for the SDP; for Blair's 'New Labour' a few times; and then wasted my vote on the Liberals before ending up voting for a rebel Tory. I now sit at a crossroads looking at a morally bankrupt Conservative party and hoping that a sensible Labour party springs back into life. In short, I have been very promiscuous with my political allegiances over the best part of forty years. I could be called a political dilettante or a pragmatic short-term thinker, but in truth I'm looking for the vision and competence to reconcile the two questions underpinning our politics.

Living through the slow then sudden collapse of communism, my generation came to economics via osmosis. We had seen wage and price controls fail before in the seventies, but a whole political and economic system crashing was clearly a seismic event. The great communist experiment had visibly failed and we were left with different forms of capitalism. The Soviet experiment had led to hunger, misery and social stagnation and all because planned economies didn't work. They didn't work because they missed the self-interest and striving dynamic that underpinned growth in liberal democracies. I don't know if it was true that Soviet factories could produce a glut of left-footed shoes and a major shortage of right-footed shoes, but this type of story became emblematic of communism's failure – helped by a media preying on and perpetuating long-held prejudices.

It is argued that, without the profit motive, people have no reason to work, optimise resources or improve the current situation. It comes down to human nature which, at a national level, brings either success or failure – we are selfish animals and not disposed to work collectively with our fellow man, unless there is something in it for us. Capitalism has essentially won, even if it changes or evolves, and it will always be based on the principle that rewarding self-interest is best for society as a whole – unequal, for sure, but the cake is bigger so everyone should benefit. Under Thatcher, the old Keynesian consensus was superseded by monetarism, deregulation and breaking of the unions. The driving force was to give individuals freedom to act and be rewarded accordingly, certainly not to build a robust welfare state. There was also the more insidious principle that society should not have to support the lazy or feckless who are looking for something for nothing.

While most governments have seen the need for a safety net, more right-wing administrations have aggressively used the 'scrounger versus responsible striver' argument. The go-to rhetoric of most politicians is to support 'hard-working families', thereby drawing a distinction with those who don't work hard and emphasising the family unit as society's category of choice.

The Blair/Brown government espoused a softer form of social democracy but it was still predicated on economic growth, using capitalist principles, albeit with better redistribution of society's spoils. These policies, plus some luck, led to relatively benign economic conditions which made redistribution more palatable. Governments from 2008 onwards have ridden fiscal breakdown and austerity, a pandemic, a broadly failed economic recovery plan and, of course, Brexit and subsequent economic damage – but, broadly, they have not questioned that the selfish individual is the main driver of success. The pressing question is: can greater freedom, and feeding the capitalist beast even more, drag the whole economy to a better place, and, if so, how long will it take?

If capitalism works on a national scale, then the whole new dimension of globalisation forces us to fall back even more on self-interest. Our country needs to be competitive as it sells our goods and services pretty well anywhere in the world. We want the employment, tax receipts and community benefits that being successful brings. We incentivise and encourage our companies and institutions to strive to win internationally, and we reward management and shareholders, despite the fact that the power of global organisations has quietly sucked agency away from the individual and the nation-state.

Capitalism has done me huge favours in my life and I have no intention of trashing the principles. I'm very confident that companies I've been employed by would not have worked so hard to improve their biscuits or baby food if the profit motive had not been there – or if there hadn't been a risk of someone else coming in with a better offer and stealing the business. For a planned economy to achieve these things, progress would at best be patchy and probably wouldn't happen – which in a global economy would be a slow form of suicide.

I've witnessed the effects of globalisation first-hand and have participated in decisions that affect thousands of lives, such as in which country to site a new factory. In some businesses, production has been moved offshore, to countries like China, where labour is cheaper, meaning that the UK can win against a slew of international competitors. This clearly has geopolitical implications, and should be challenged for other reasons, but we are still seeing the unintended positive consequences of Adam Smith's 'invisible hand' on markets, and on a massive scale.

As well as multinationals, I've also worked in private equity which is in the vanguard of capitalism. The argument in favour of private equity is that it enables businesses to fight on a national and international level, but it's also ruthless, driven by the aligned self-interest of backers and managements – of which I was one, although I'd distance myself from the brutal asset-stripping and questionable financial engineering which, without regulation, are a logical consequence of right-wing economic policies.

If self-interested capitalism leads to a bigger economic cake for all, then the other big question is about how you divide that cake fairly. Do it too evenly, the argument goes, and you have to tax the income-generators, which reduces the incentive to generate income and in turn reduces the cake. This is a ludicrous over-simplification but, nevertheless, the debate is underpinned by this principle. In their excellent book, *The Spirit Level*, Pickett and Wilkinson dissect and analyse equality, and, by extension, inequality, in a wide range of countries around the world. The evidence is pretty irrefutable that excessive inequality is a function of many liberal democracies, with the UK being especially high. Evidence also clearly shows that societies with improved levels of equality are more successful – as measured by life expectancy, health, education, crime and general happiness. Equality has a significantly better correlation to these measurements than GDP per capita – so maybe the amount of money in my pocket compared to my neighbour's might not be the key driver of my wellbeing? This may weaken the argument for allowing capitalism to run free but it doesn't support the counter-argument for planned economies, as they come without a solution for motivating self-interest. The other interesting outcome was that large numbers of people would support a movement to greater equality, at least in principle. Of course, the weakness of this may well be in the execution of relevant policies where money is taken out of some people's pockets to give to others, or spent on socially advantageous projects like hospitals and roads.

In our mature western European economies, we still want health, facilities for an ageing population, national security, infrastructure, education and a raft of other socially desirable investments. Some of these can be handled by the private sector but many are best controlled centrally because the profit motivator has proven to have unintended and detrimental consequences. If the private sector is involved, they will want to be paid, because they want to make a profit which will, in turn, exacerbate inequality, because only some can pay. Greater or, at least fairer, redistribution of wealth means taxing the better off and either giving the money to the less well off or ploughing it into desired social services.

A couple of the Nordic countries have managed to address inequality by reducing the pay differences between jobs, but this is helped by their historical legacy. It would be difficult, though not impossible, to implement this from a standing start in an environment like the United Kingdom. Increasing pay rates for public sector workers would drag other low-paid workers up over time, though clearly inflation will be the big beast to tackle, even if helped by greater productivity. This would be 'bubble-up' rather than 'trickle-down' economics; the theory is predicated on the fact that for every new pound low-income citizens earn, a high proportion goes back into the economy – enhancing the multiplier effect of new money.

If a bigger cake means more inequality but greater equality improves life, we need to engage in a debate about how to square this circle, where the key measure is quality of life. This needs an understanding of how different people think about these things and a starting premise that most people are good and well-meaning – moving away from the conflictual, right versus left paradigm. At the very least, we can learn to disagree more effectively by understanding the biases of the opponent. In my mind, the key variable is fairness and how we interpret it. For some, and mostly on the left of politics, it's about equality and making all as equal as possible, regardless of skills or risk. They would argue that it is a selfish society that assesses a merchant banker as significantly more valuable than a nurse, even though the latter may save your life; it is a selfish society that allows people to live in poverty while others have superyachts.

The other major distinction around fairness is the pay gap

between men and women. On a like-for-like job basis, women are moving towards, or have achieved, parity, but it's been a battle over many generations – right up to Asda shop workers in 2021 (mainly women) winning a Supreme Court judgment for pay equal to that of Asda warehouse workers (mainly men). Women, on average, get paid significantly less than men, in large part due to the propensity for more part-time work and our social structures around caring, household or child-rearing responsibilities. Inequality is built to the system for women, and it is an unfair fight against the patriarchy history and society's attitudes. The consequences of all this are that fairness demands that the rich pay more and that the spoils are spread out more evenly across the population.

We then bounce back to the economic efficiency argument. The alternative, and more right-wing, view of fairness focuses on the freedom to earn. This perspective is more about proportionality; it recognises inequality, but prioritises the opportunity for wealth generation, according to an artificial valuation of ability, together with an appetite for risk. Linked directly to this is a different view of unfairness, arguing that it is unfair that people should be prevented from exploiting their skills to optimise their wealth. I've deliberately taken out the concept of 'hard work' as a measure of value, though it is sometimes used unthinkingly as a justification for wealth differential. There is precious little evidence that different groups in society work harder than others. Moreover, the low-paid typically suffer from longer hours and more anti-social conditions, especially in economically difficult times – as seen in the austerity world post-2012.

There are other powerful influences on our thinking about equality, like adherence to our tribe, respect for authority or rules, compassion and a deep understanding of the reciprocity that successful societies need. Many people freely offer their time and money for community activities, giving the lie to the pure concept of 'homo-economicus'. We are not always highly rational, making crass calculations about our own self-interest – our homes, villages and nations give an emotional succour that we don't put a price on. Our human relationships have an intrinsic value which we can set against pure economic wealth. I always marvel at the argument that if we don't pay top managers international salaries, we will lose them to Frankfurt or New York. Some will go for sure, but don't these people have kids in school, a partner that doesn't speak German, or a Sunday morning cricket practice to organise? I've always been suspicious that these are self-serving arguments that drive even greater inequality.

At the top of this essay, I argued that, in the universe of national politics, there are two main planets: economic efficiency and social equality. The first tries and fails to have the certainty of the natural sciences, and the second is heavily influenced by our human natures, both conscious and unconscious. However, there are other moons that circle the two planets, pulling different economic tides at different times. The shifts may be geopolitical or structural, such as membership of the EU; they may reshape national borders via devolution or independence; and they may be driven by the motivations and ideas of leaders. But most elections are fought on the economy or how to spread the nation's wealth, and for good reason, because that affects more of us than, say, a Falklands war, or dodgy politicians with questionable morals – though, electorally, Brexit is a rip-tide of an exception.

My hope is that people will recognise the importance of the economic/social dilemma and appreciate that it's a debate that should be encouraged – and encouraged in the spirit that most people are decent. It is unhelpful to label people 'pinko tree huggers' or 'rabid mill-owners'. Most of us come with prejudices, for sure, but most of us are well-meaning – it's just that where some of us see a six, others will always see a nine. We also approach the debates with different agendas, and different degrees of self-interest and altruism. Many of us would find it a challenge to understand and evaluate these in our own heads, let alone in the heads of someone sitting opposite us.

Where I come out at the end of all this is that I think we have probably lost sight of the necessary balance in our society. The United Kingdom is too unequal and that is bad for everyone. I want my kids to grow up in a country without bubbling resentment and where everyone has an equal chance to be the best they can be.

The safety net in our society must be protected at all costs and cannot be expected to operate efficiently on a threadbare basis – our society is rich enough to look after the significantly disadvantaged. I don't know many people who, having come out of hospital after a life-threatening problem, still advocate reducing investment in the NHS. And who would credibly oppose greater wage parity between men and women?

I'm convinced that the profit motive, well controlled, is best for us all, because it grows the cake – but I've recently developed some serious misgivings about the role of globalisation. It needs thoughtful (not Trumpian) solutions and I really wish I knew how to solve it. I suspect there needs to be a movement back towards a more social democratic ideology, but one adapted to the current societal and geopolitical environment. I'm keeping a weather eye on the new Teal movement in Australia, because I can see something interesting in their environmental and more conservative economic policies. They just need to factor in a greater degree of social equality. Enlightened policies in New Zealand and some of the Nordic countries also have valuable lessons for us.

Right now, this is where I stand and I'm scanning around for a home for my vote. So, if anyone has a better idea for how to generate the conditions in which the two planets of economic efficiency and social equality can spin in perfect harmony, please make yourself known. I'll throw off my dilettante cloak and become a disciple.

Tilting at Windmills

We accidentally bought a seventeenth-century, thirty-nine foot, twenty-five ton garden ornament, which also happened to be the country's oldest working post-mill. It was attached to a stable block that had planning permission for a three-bedroomed house. What started as a money-making venture ended up with my business partner and I owning a piece of English history and an example of engineering brilliance that, given its period of construction, is truly awe-inspiring. It is said that Outwood Mill was built by people escaping the Great Plague in 1665 and that from its top they could see the glow from the Great Fire of London in 1666. The whole thing is built around a great baulk of oak which was transported on oxen-driven carts from seven miles away, raised and hand tooled to be the centre of the mill. The main body of the mill was then turned around this trunk in order to catch the necessary wind. The sails, which can be shuttered closed or open, then connect via a cog and gear system to the vertical drive – essentially a thick, straight spindle that turns by the power of the wind and slots into the top runner stone. Wheat is fed into the runner stone which then grinds it against the bottom bed-stone, releasing the flour by way of channels cut into the stone. Wholemeal flour can then be adapted, bagged or stored before distributing to the local community. Almost all of the construction was made of wood, which is pretty much how it remains today – many of the moving parts and structures are the original pieces from nearly three hundred and sixty years ago. Sadly, a bag of flour milled here now would cost about three times what you'd pay in the supermarket, but in a post-apocalyptic world we will be quids in and sitting pretty.

The other feature, as yet overlooked by historians, is that a windmill is a great place for a piss-up. You haven't lived until you have played chicken with a fast-approaching sail as you hop in and out of the roundhouse door – which is built for someone the size of a hobbit. The other iteration of this game is to lie down under the path of the sail and hope you are not too fat to be clipped or decapitated.

One of my friends memorably observed that, while a piss-up normally ends with a drunken game of *Twister*, being able to fire up a windmill takes the entertainment to another level. That night must have ended spectacularly, because when I woke in the morning, I found my cowboy boots attached to the top sail, fifty feet above my head. I do hope our forefathers had similar fun.

It's more than just a huge garden ornament. It's something beautiful and immensely practical, designed by people who had real talent and engineering skill. It doesn't need regular software updates and has worked for hundreds of years without a reboot. It was the centre of a community operating an early form of socialism and is a living part of our history. What's not to like?

I leave you with an anonymous poem, written in the 1950s in honour of Outwood Windmill.

In sixteen hundred and sixty six,
When London was burning like rotten sticks,
To tell the news to the neighbouring farms,
I, the Windmill, swung wide my arms.

The wind blew high on this Surrey down
And fanned the fire in the crumbling town.
Folk cried, "It will burn till the great wind calms".
(And wildly and wildly I turned my arms).

How the timber crashed! There were terrible falls.
London Bridge went and the great St Paul's,
The folk gathered round me and were filled with alarms,
But I stuck to my post, and I swung my arms.

I'm not quite the mill that once I used to be
When I swung my arms for the world to see,
For those were the days of my youth, you know,
Now nearly three hundred years ago.

Buying a Watch
Really Shouldn't be this Difficult

For a few years, I've been looking for a replacement to an old sports watch which sadly expired through overuse. My criteria are simple, in that it needs to be waterproof, have normal watch hands, rather than a digital display, and a light so it can be read in the dark. The light is the most important thing, not because I want to dive around shipwrecks at night, which, in truth, would scare the crap out of me, but because I need to be able to judge whether my bladder will last to the end in a cinema or theatre. 'Use your phone,' I hear you shout – but if I do that people around me tut, and my wife rolls her eyes in despair. It's a middle-age problem, as yet untapped by the multi-million-pound watch industry.

I've trawled the market, online and offline, and have bemused many a shop assistant with, what seems to me, a very reasonable request. As an aside, I've never met a watch salesperson who has the first clue about the functions of their watches – they just look it up on the internet while you are standing there. Eventually, I found a Casio which looked like it might do the job, and my original watch was a Casio, so the stars were starting to align. It had hands, a button that said 'light' and was euphemistically called a sports watch. I took the plunge and bought it off their website, though I have to admit to a dull sense of misgiving.

When it arrived, I left it by the front door for a couple of days, given my fundamental suspicion of anything vaguely to do with technology. I have a negative force field around me that scrabbles electronic devices, disrupting the user interfaces that most people happily and successfully enjoy – it's a force that follows me outside the house and infects perfectly straightforward machines like parking-ticket dispensers or supermarket scanners. But this time I had a stern word with myself, and smuggled it into the office to dedicate time to getting it to work – without the rest of the family being able to judge my possible failure.

Firstly, the hands on the face could not be operated by a simple knob on the side as you would expect. Oh no! It needed to be fucking-well programmed to one of fifty worldwide cities – all with a short code that I found in the back of a hundred-page instruction manual. So TOK on the digital display actually meant Tokyo and I needed to get to LON. Having established this, I then had to understand the function of the four buttons on the watch, though they were helpfully named things like 'mode' and 'adjust'. What was less helpful was that the instructions referred to buttons named A, B, C, and D but didn't actually put a letter to a button – well, it did, but not until page 17, by which time I was standing on the window ledge, considering my next step. Having established the lettering sequence, I then had to press the buttons in a convoluted order, something akin to a game of *Twister* for your fingers. At one stage, I had two fingers holding down two buttons and tried using my nose to get the third required button to release its secrets. No! I was still stuck with TOK, though there was the enticing prospect to come of a stopwatch, an alarm and a second time-zone setting, should I be too lazy to move the hands forward or back. I persevered for another half an hour, finally resorting to holding all four buttons down in hundreds of different combinations, while feeling the prick of tears at the back of my eyes. Even if I actually managed to set it properly, the chances were just above zero of me doing it again when the clocks changed or I was abroad. I was wrapped in misery, self-loathing and anger: misery because I'd wasted so much time; self-loathing because I constantly fail at this type of thing; and anger because I have learned to give technology time and yet it still defeated me. At my lowest point, I questioned how I would ever survive in a world where technology is going to be so all encompassing. I started to fantasise about living in a Dickensian household of log fires, leather-bound books and jaunty carriage drivers called Barkis. It's important to be fairly rich in historical fantasies!

Anyway, the watch was discreetly packed up and smuggled into my car, before going to the post office. I needed to get rid of it as quickly as possible, otherwise it would sit there judging me. I enclosed a snotty letter to Casio and felt a huge relief that I would never see it again – or would I?

The extraordinary thing is that I now remember that I had bought the same Casio watch a couple of years previously. Then I failed to get past Denver (DEN) in the city programme and sent it back to Casio with a similar snotty note. Somewhere in my head, there is clearly an established neural pathway that has made me do the exact same stupid thing: a neural pathway that goes dormant after disaster before opening up again when the burning desire for a watch with a light re-emerges. Buying a watch is a relatively benign activity, of course, but men do seem to have a propensity to repeat mistakes if our desires overcome our common-sense – from repeating mistakes in choosing partners to repeating the 'never again' binge-drinking session. This mistake cost me seventy pounds and some angst, but others can exact a much higher price.

I've spent a lot of my adult life trying not to keep making the same mistakes over and over again. It feels the grown-up thing to do, yet my family, and an honest appraisal of my time on the planet, would tell you otherwise – I consistently piss my kids off with the same conversations that always lead to door-slamming; I should never buy clothes on my own, because I always expect to lose weight, and so buy a size below; and I still order crab in a restaurant even though it consistently tastes like cat food! Maybe it's just part of a constant battle between our need for patterns which, even if foolish, anchor us, and the rational person within who just has too much to think about.

Global supply chains and product development have a lot to answer for, leading to a lowest common denominator approach – things have to work for everyone and therefore never fully satisfy anyone. Notwithstanding my technical buffoonery, it would be lovely to have products that delight, come fully formed (without an Allen key) and can simply, in one language, explain how they work – I'd pay good money for that.

So, I hang my head in shame, write a Post-it note reminding me not to buy another Casio watch, and resolve to try harder with technology. A Dickensian world seems unlikely, unless I join the House of Lords, and I do, grudgingly, rather like my iPhone, even if I can only use about ten percent of its functionality.

The Peacock Whisperer

Like vast numbers of the British population, I recently bought a live peacock. It was one of those things that seemed a good idea at the time.

I bought him as a friend for the original 'Percy the Peacock', who had lived in our small, wooded hamlet for a few years, but whose behaviour had been getting progressively worse: he was attacking his own reflection on shiny cars, leaving scratches on paintwork; he'd been found on the kitchen units in one house enjoying an impromptu breakfast; and he was caught strutting around on someone's bed in an open bungalow. His worst crime, though, was calling out for a non-existent mate, from about three in the morning to sunrise, and due to this and his wandering nature, he had managed to piss off most of the neighbours. A horny peacock makes a terrible noise when it's outside your bedroom window early in the morning.

But he was the most magnificent creature with a fabulous display of tail feathers in the mating season. He would wander from garden to garden showing us all his wares, and had been known to lead a procession of frustrated drivers, as he walked regally down the road between his regular food stops. His relationship with our chickens was mixed; normally they just tolerated each other, except when there was scattered corn to be had. Then he would puff himself up to his full magnificence and charge – even big, bad Bluebell wasn't going to take him on. Our corn bill doubled but at least we were able to ask friends, 'doesn't everyone have a peacock?'

I'm more of a doer than a thinker, so I decided that we needed to find a solution for Percy – one that would rehabilitate him with at least half of the neighbours, while knocking the corners off his worst behaviour. So, I read about it, called the government department for peacock husbandry and talked to a breeder who called herself Sussanne Peacock (at least, that's what she comes up as on my phone; I might have made her up). It seemed that it was no good buying a female, as they tend to lay their eggs on the ground, meaning that they are quickly eaten by foxes. What I needed was another male for company and they would get on famously – and it just so happened that Sussanne had one spare. Clearly the cure for a territorial, horny male bird is to get another male to share nicely. But, as I say, I'm more of a doer, so I just paid for him and had him delivered the next day. Having gone down this path, I had to then indulge in shuttle diplomacy with half of the neighbours, who may have spotted the flaw in the plan; the other half of the community were enthusiastic participants in the venture. The advice was to keep the new bird in a cage for six weeks, so he wouldn't fly off, and to introduce Percy from outside the fencing. Three or four of us requisitioned an old garage, and built an outsized cage on the front to give him some air. Then we organised a rota for feeding and general checking-in. He was named Ronnie, after Ronaldo, due to his long, elegant neck.

By now the cost of the bird, delivery, fencing hire and food was well in excess of £200 and this was starting to get the feel of a folly.

However, we stuck to it and six weeks after arrival we had a small coming-out party for Ronnie. Percy was invited and indulgently strutted around while Ronnie got used to his new freedom. It was going to be a success and for a week they did indeed play nicely, even though it was clear that Percy was the Alpha male.

And then it wasn't a success – Percy had had enough of his new mate, who may have turned into a rival. Ronnie was unceremoniously chased out of the woods. By now, I was nearly fluent in peacock so I scoured the local area making plaintive, cawing noises to tempt him back – should you find yourself in this position, YouTube also do a version for your phone if you're too embarrassed to do it yourself. Ronnie was not to be found but at least the neighbours refused my offer to reimburse their investment. Incidentally, all this was going on at one of the craziest and most high profile periods in my working life, so I can claim that I wasn't really thinking straight.

The story ends happily, though. After week of cycling around the area, cawing like the village idiot, I got a response. It turned out that Ronnie had found some other peacocks in a local country house with large gardens, and all was well with his world. Percy's behaviour, however, deteriorated, culminating in him actively trying to shag someone else's chickens. He'd tried and failed with the pheasants, who were quicker than chickens. It was decided, by a cabal of residents, that he had to go and, as my reputation as a peacock whisperer was badly dented, I had little say in the matter. He was captured humanely, with a blanket, and then relocated to a huge country estate with a gamekeeper and some other peacocks, including females – yippee!

It all worked out well and I learned some valuable lessons along the way. Do better research, and don't listen to someone who has a male peacock to sell. Remember my O-level biology and apply it to mummy and daddy peacock husbandry. Perhaps a better vocabulary in peacock could have facilitated a better outcome? It was a typical project for me – doing it and then worrying about the consequences, though I did manage to rope in several willing accomplices. I then had to rely on my normal style of apologising charmingly, offering to pay and moving on to the next idea. Hopefully, I have more successes than failures in such projects but *caveat emptor*, as they say in these parts. Whatever... harmony has returned to our little square of England, though I do really miss Percy. He was a magnificent bird with a cocksure personality and I just hope that soon there will be lots of little Percies out there, ready to terrorise the neighbourhoods of the future.

I Want a Viking Burial

I have the idea that I'd like a full Viking burial when my time comes. Not a gentle, hushed affair in the crematorium, followed by sausages on a stick and warm Prosecco at the local hotel.

What I have in mind is a ten- or twelve-foot longboat made out of Somerset willow, with a prow at each end. Clearly the front should be something fierce like a gargoyle, but maybe a chicken at the back would add an element of whimsy. Some shields along each side would be nice and a sail with an exotic typeface saying 'Valhalla or Bust'. I would then be laid out on a bed of straw, arms crossed over my chest and wearing my best Viking outfit – especially a horned helmet that will make me look kind of tough.

I've identified a suitable launch beach, down on the Gower Peninsula, which has a particularly awkward set of steps down to the slipway for the pallbearers to navigate. This will add the element of comedy so often lacking in modern-day funerals. I will be naming my pallbearers beforehand and allocating positions – all the small guys on one side and the tall guys on the other, just to complete the fun – and I will be strapped in (under my tunic) by Thule luggage straps.

Then to the serious bit: the launch. I don't think I trust any of my friends to fire a burning arrow accurately and the prospect of drifting off into the Bristol Channel before landing in Weston-Super-Mare is not good. We will have to tie firelighters to sticks, so my eighty-year-old pallbearers can solemnly light the straw, as they battle a four-foot beach break coming off Langland Head. I have always been struck by the Kirk Douglas film *The Vikings*, when they are sent off with mournful horn playing in the background – it would be a very nice touch if someone could learn to play the whale-bone horn before the event.

There are a few practicalities for my family to manage, as the government takes a pretty dim view of this kind of thing. I do have a friend who is a doctor, an experienced sailor and is qualified to bury people at sea, though I suspect this is not what the BMA had in mind when he was certified. There are a few compromises that can be made but I'm loath to give too much ground at this stage.

There is a serious point somewhere in this piece, though it's well-hidden. A funeral shouldn't be a treadmill, where the major concession to individuality is not having to wear black. We should be able to celebrate our lives and deaths in personal ways, and I'm glad we are starting to see more humanist- and celebrant-led events. I'm not especially religious and I suspect that when the lights go out, that is it, though I don't want to burn any bridges with whatever religion or deity happens to have got it right. With any luck, it might just be Odin!

Today I played Pooh Sticks against my son and lost –
I'm getting better at handling the gut-wrenching disappointment.

David (aged 732 months)

Useful Reading

Cherry, Kendra *The Big Five Personality Traits*
https://www.verywellmind.com/the-big-five-personality-
dimensions-2795422#toc-agreeableness (2021)

Clark, Cory J. et al *Tribalism is Human Nature*
https://journals-sagepub-com (2019)

Foot, Hugh & McCreaddie, May *The Handbook of Communication Skills*
Routledge (2006)

Gregg. J *Laughter Is Good Medicine* Oregon State University (2002)

Haidt, Jonathan *The Righteous Mind: Why Good People are Divided by
Politics & Religion* Penguin Books Ltd (2012)
Haidt, Jonathan *Polarised | The Psychology of Tribalism*
https://www.youtube.com/watch?v=3zjKU6r0-Vc (2020)

Hertz, Noreena *Talking Politics: The Politics of Loneliness*
https://noreena.com/the-politics-of-loneliness/ (2020)

Jablonka, Ivan *A History of Masculinity* Penguin Random House (2023)

Liddon, Louise & Barry, John *Perspectives in Male Psychology: An Introduction* Wiley Blackwell (2021)

Martin, Rod A. *The Psychology of Humor: An Integrative Approach* Elsevier Science & Technology (2006)

McAvoy, Jean *Exposing the Authoritarian Personality* in *Investigating Psychology* Brace, Nicola & Byford, Jovan (eds) Oxford University Press / The Open University (2012)

Orwell, George *Notes on Nationalism* first published in *Polemic: October1945* https://www.orwellfoundation.com

Pickett, Kate and Wilkinson, Richard G. *The Spirit Level: Why More Equal Societies Almost Always Do Better* Allen Lane (2009)

Power, Nina *What Do Men Want?* Penguin Random House (2022)

Vianello, M., Schnabel, K., Sriram, N., & Nosek, B. *Gender Differences in Implicit and Explicit Personality Traits.* https://www.sciencedirect.com/science/article/abs/pii/S0191886913007836 (2013)

Webb, Richard E & Rosenbaum, Philip J *Tribalism: Where George Orwell Leads Us and Where An Understanding of Existential-Relational Positions Extends Us* https://journals.sagepub.com (2021)

Weisberg, Yanna J., DeYoung, Colin G., & Hirsh, Jacob B. *Gender Differences in Personality Across the Ten Aspects of the Big Five* https://www.frontiersin.org/articles (2011)

Constellations Press is a small independent press
committed to publishing works of fiction, memoir and essays.

We publish books that boldly reimagine society, and
that celebrate our diverse humanity, adding to the
total sum of the world's beauty.

constellationspress.co.uk